A Theory of Psychological Scaling

A THEORY OF
PSYCHOLOGICAL SCALING

CLYDE H. COOMBS
Associate Professor of Psychology
University of Michigan

GREENWOOD PRESS, PUBLISHERS
WESTPORT, CONNECTICUT

Library of Congress Cataloging in Publication Data

Coombs, Clyde Hamilton, 1912-
   A theory of psychological scaling.

   Reprint of the ed. published by the Engineering
Research Institute, University of Michigan, Ann Arbor, which was issued as the institute's Bulletin
no. 34.
   Bibliography: p.
   1. Psychometrics. I. Title. II. Series:
Michigan. University. Research Institute. Engineering research bulletin ; no. 34. [DNLM: 1. Psychometrics. BF39 C776t 1952a]
[BF39.C64 1976] 620'.008s [152.8]   75-41413
ISBN 0-8371-8646-3

Copyright 1952 The University of Michigan

Originally published in 1951 by Engineering Research Institute,
University of Michigan, Ann Arbor

Reprinted with the permission of Clyde H. Coombs

Reprinted in 1976 by Greenwood Press,
a division of Williamhouse-Regency Inc.

Library of Congress Catalog Card Number 75-41413

ISBN 0-8371-8646-3

Printed in the United States of America

To
L. L. Thurstone and **Warner Brown**

TABLE OF CONTENTS

PREFACE

This monograph describes the construction of a psychological theory which defines the information contained in the responses of individuals to stimuli. This has been accomplished by abstracting certain properties of behavior which are invariant over content. These have been classified and quantified in a theory of data which, with the quasi-formal basis hypothesized here, determines the genotypic inferences which may be made from manifest behavior.

On the basis presented here certain theoretical concepts and interpretations are developed and also certain new experimental procedures and experimental relations presented.

There are a number of further implications and practical developments of this system which are the outgrowth of a course on the theory of scaling at the University of Michigan. Publication of this latter material is dependent upon the prior publication of this monograph, but an indication of these further developments is contained in (11).

The general theory has been in the process of formation over a period of four years, and to a very considerable degree it represents the work of others than myself, In it᷑ very earliest formative stages it was exposed to the criticisms of Professors S. A. Stouffer, C. F. Mosteller, P. Lazarsfeld, and Mr. B. W. White as part of a Rand project in the Laboratory of Social Relations at Harvard University. In the three years since then the theory has undergone continuous modification and development in response to the criticisms and suggestions of students and colleagues in the course on the theory of scaling and in two concurrent seminars, one on the theory of psychological measurement, the other on the application of mathematics to the social sciences. It is to be anticipated that the theory will undergo additional changes both in its abstract and its real aspects as additional work is done with it. Its presentation now is necessary for the presentation of certain consequences of practical interest to psychologists and social scientists. However, the development of further consequences and the generalization to multidimensional space will undoubtedly result in changes in the basis.

To list all the people from whose criticisms and suggestions I have benefited is next to impossible, but to the following particularly I wish to express my appreciation of many benefits gained from their sustained interest, encouragement, and criticism: Dr. George Austin, Dr. Joseph F. Bennett, Professor John Carroll, Professor Irving Copi, Professor Leon Festinger, Professor Max Hutt, Professor Donald Marquis, Professor Theodore Newcomb, Dr. Howard Raiffa, and Professor Robert M. Thrall.

I wish especially to acknowledge my appreciation of the aid I have received from Mr. John Milholland, my research assistant for the past two years, who did much of the experimental work presented in Chapters VII and VIII, and who was of continual assistance in all phases of the work.

It should be unnecessary to point out that none of these people have any responsibility for such inadequacies and defects as may remain.

This research has been supported by a grant from the Board of Governors of The Horace H. Rackham School of Graduate Studies, University of Michigan, and currently under ONR Contract Nonr-374(00), NR 041-011/1-29-51 for a project on the mathematics of measurement by partial ordering, a joint contract of Professor Robert M. Thrall of the Department of Mathematics and myself, administered by the Engineering Research Institute of the University of Michigan.

I am indebted to Professor A. E. White, Director of the Engineering Research Institute, for making available publication funds, and to Dr. B. A. Uhlendorf, Editor of the Institute, for preparing the manuscript for publication.

Clyde H. Coombs

University of Michigan
January, 1952

Chapter I

SOME ASPECTS OF THE METHATHEORY
OF MEASUREMENT

There are two major aspects to every theory of measurement; on the one hand, there is the formal, logical aspect, and on the other hand, the experimental or operational side. By the formal or logical aspect is meant a set of axioms which specify operations and relationships among a set of elements. By the experimental or operational side is meant a set of operations on the objects themselves by means of which they can be observed, in respect to some attribute, to satisfy certain axioms. These two aspects correspond respectively to what Woodger[25] calls structure and meaning, or alternatively syntax and semantics.

As a consequence of the fact that operations on objects do not always reveal the same axioms to be satisfied, there has gradually developed a series of what are called scales, each scale corresponding in principle, to a set of axioms. If it is possible to perform operations on objects such that the objects are observed to satisfy the axioms of one of the scales, then the entire mathematical development based on those axioms may be validly substituted for operations on the objects.

The development of physics as "the queen of the sciences" may be regarded as a consequence, in part, of two fundamental conditions: (1) the development of a powerful mathematics built on the axioms of arithmetic, and (2) the fact that these axioms appear to be realized in vast areas of physical phenomena. Consequently, scientists in other areas of knowledge, and in particular social scientists, have not only respected physics but have tried to build their own science in its image. Unfortunately, the second condition above is, in general, not satisfied by social psychological phenomena. It behooves the social scientist to try to formulate axiom systems which satisfy the behavior he is interested in and to encourage the development of the appropriate mathematics. In its broadest sense, then, this is simply the recommendation that the social scientist attend to his measurement theory.

To return to the subject of the different scales of measurement, S. S. Stevens[21] recognizes four scales of measurement, the ratio scale, the interval scale, the ordinal scale, and the nominal scale. There is no one place in the literature in which the axioms for these scales are given, certainly not in a systematic fashion. Axioms for the ratio and ordinal scales are most clearly stated by Nagel,[20] who gives twelve axioms of quantity. The first six generate an ordinal scale and the entire twelve generate a ratio scale. Alternative postulational bases for an interval scale are contained in the first chapter of Von Neumann and Morgenstern's *Theory of Games and Economic Behavior*[24] and in J. Marschak's recent paper in *Econometrica.*[18] It would be desirable to formulate a single set of axioms such that each scale could be characterized by a subset of these axioms, then the logical distinctions between the scales would be clear. In the summary of one of the sessions of a seminar on the application of mathematics to the social sciences, there is contained such a set of axioms prepared by Dr. Howard Raiffa. One of the natural consequences of the abstract approach is that it generates other types of scales not previously recognized experimentally or theoretically.

Interesting differences between these scales occur with respect to the assignment of numbers in the process of measurement. If the axioms for a ratio scale are satisfied by an attribute, the assignment of any one number to any one object is sufficient for fixing a unique number for each of all the other objects. This is equivalent to the selection of a unit of measurement. If the axioms for an interval scale are satisfied by an attribute, the assignment of any two different numbers to any two different objects is sufficient to fix a unique number for each of all the other objects with respect to this attribute. This is equivalent to the selection of an origin and a unit of measurement. It is evident that for an interval scale the differences between the numbers assigned to objects form a ratio scale. If the axioms for an ordinal scale are satisfied, the assignment of any number to any one object fixes an upper bound or a lower bound for the number to be assigned to any other object, and no other knowledge about the number for any other object is contained in the measurement. In the case of a nominal scale, the assignment of a number to an object or class of equal objec merely uses up that number and puts no other constraint on the assignment of other numbers to other classes of objects.

There are a number of useful psychological scales which may be added to Stevens' list. Among these is the type of scale called an ordered metric,[8] in which the order of objects on a continuum is known, and also the distances between objects may themselves be at least partially ordered. It is evident that this type of scale is weaker than an interval scale but more powerful than an ordinal scale. With this type of scale, the assignment of any two different numbers to a *particular pair* of objects (the two adjacent ones that are farthest apart) fixes a pair of numbers for every other object, one an upper bound and the other a lower bound.

Another type of scale which can be added to the system is the partially ordered scale. For immediate purposes it suffices to say that it is useful in the treatment of intransitive paired comparisons or, more generally, what will be called conjunctive and disjunctive behavior as distinct from summative behavior.[10] It is evident that the partially ordered scale falls between an ordinal and a nominal scale. The assignment of any number to any one object in a partially ordered system provides either an upper or a lower bound for the number to be assigned to *some* other objects.

From a study of these scales it is evident that they may be ordered on the basis of the axioms they satisfy. The ratio scale satisfies the most axioms and may be regarded as the most powerful scale. The interval scale comes next, then the ordinal scale, and, finally, the nominal scale is the weakest. The axioms satisfied by one of these scales are included in the axioms satisfied by a more powerful scale and include those satisfied by a weaker scale. Thus, an interval scale is also an ordinal and a nominal scale, and a ratio scale includes them all.

A more complete listing of scales, however, reveals that they are partially ordered. This is made evident by regarding scales as being composite scales. A scale may be regarded as constituted of two kinds of elements, the objects themselves and the distances between objects. The objects may be scaled on a nominal, partially ordered, or ordered scale, for example. The distances between objects, regarded as elements, may also be scaled on one of these scales. Listing the scale that holds for the objects themselves, first, and the scale that holds for the distances between objects, second, the scale called here a nominal scale may be regarded as a nominal-nominal scale. The partially ordered scale becomes a partially ordered-nominal scale. The ordinal scale is seen to be an ordinal-nominal scale. The ordered metric includes the ordinal-partially ordered, and the ordinal-ordinal.

3

On this basis a lattice of scales would consist of the following:

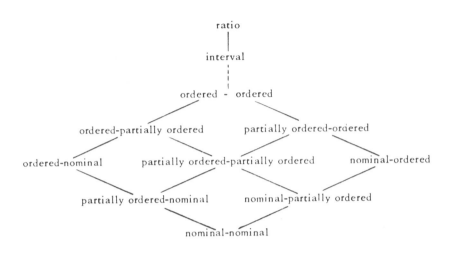

where a connecting line between two scales indicates that the axioms of the lower scale are included in the axioms of the higher scale. Referring to the distances or intervals between objects as first-order differences, the above lattice is constructed on zero and first-order differences between objects. This lattice could be extended by including second-order differences between objects, which could be elements of an abstract system and on which there could also be relations such as "greater than." Thus, an example of a second-order difference relation would be the statement that the difference between the distances between stimuli A and B and stimuli B and C is greater than the differences between the distances between stimuli C and D and stimuli D and E.

The relation of the interval scale to the ordered-ordered is complex. Mr. Donald Mela has pointed out* that if the number of stimuli is infinite, the ordered-ordered scale is identical with the interval scale. But if the number of stimuli is finite, it would require an infinite succession of differences between differences to make them identical.

Elsewhere,[10] an arbitrary distinction has been drawn, for purposes of exposition, between psychological measurement and psychological scaling on the basis of the axioms that are satisfied. In brief, if the operations of arithmetic are permissible on the scale elements, i.e.,

---

*Personal communication.

4

numbers, assigned to objects or their differences, these scales are classified as measurement; otherwise they are classified as scaling. On this basis, ratio and interval scales are both classified as measurement, and the remaining scales, including the ordered metric, ordinal scale, partially ordered scale, and nominal scale are classified as scaling. The distinction is arbitrary but convenient. In the broadest sense, however, all scales represent degrees of measurement, a ratio scale representing the highest degree, a nominal scale the lowest, and the other scales partially ordered between these two. This partial ordering of the scales themselves on degree of measurement represents an ordering of the power of the scales. The more axioms of quantity that are used in the basis of a scale the more elaborate the mathematical development of the abstract system. There are more operations that can be performed on the numbers and more relations to be deduced. It is in this sense that one scale is spoken of as being more powerful than another. There is a great difference in this respect between the interval and the ordinal scales, and it is natural that psychologists have frequently been willing to make the necessary assumptions to achieve an interval scale in preference to an ordinal scale.

There is a relationship, perhaps, between the power of a scale, on the one hand, and the generality of its applicability, on the other. The more powerful the scale the more axioms it is based on. For a scale to be validly applicable, an object system must also satisfy the axioms of the scale. In general, one would expect that the more axioms the fewer the object systems that could satisfy it. Thu , the power of a system and its generality tend to be inversely related.

A characteristic of much of the development of measurement theory in psychology and the social sciences has been an effort to achieve more powerful scales without sacrificing generality. One consequence of this is that the meaning associated with the numbers has moved toward more gross statistical interpretations and away from individual interpretations. This is evident in Gulliksen's paper on paired comparisons and the logic of measurement. [13] Judgments of individuals incompatible with the general solution are regarded as discriminal error, but the prediction of the distribution of a number of judgments is frequently highly accurate.

Guttman's work in scaling theory [14] may be regarded as an effort to avoid the more gross statistical interpretations of scale values to permit interpretation of the individual case. The result is that he drops from an interval scale to an ordinal scale, from a more powerful system to a more general system.

A characteristic of the philosophy which underlies most psychological measurement theory is that it is directed toward trying to *construct* scales, to *make* scales. In the approach presented here the point of view is that the

5

existence of a scale has psychological significance[7] and that the conclusion that a scale exists cannot be drawn if the measurement technique and theory guarantees the construction of a unidimensional scale.

Chapter II

THE PROBLEM OF PSYCHOLOGICAL MEASUREMENT

The problem area with which this theory is concerned is the area of psychological measurement and scaling. It is difficult to define this area precisely, but in general terms, the problem is concerned with the magnitudes of subjective experiences and other characteristics of personal qualities: how strongly one feels about something, just how anti-X an individual is, how much of some ability he possesses.

It is immediately evident that the fundamental problem with which measurement theorists in psychology have been faced is the problem of a unit of measurement. How can a personal experience have a unit of measurement common to different persons? Serious attempts to solve this problem have taken one of two approaches: (1) relating the unit of measurement to a measurable physical attribute of stimuli by a numerical law—the classical psychophysical solution, and (2) relating the unit of measurement to a statistical concept-Thurstone's Law of Comparative Judgment.[21] The classical solution of psychophysics is based on the abscissa of the well-known psychometric function,[12] Thurstone's on the ordinate. Thurstone's Case V and the psychophysical solution both reduce to the assumption that equally often noticed differences are equal, an assumption that is not present in the complete Law of Comparative Judgment.

Several more recent attempts to "solve" the problem of a psychological unit of measurement have taken a different approach.[8,14,17] This new approach has been to solve the problem by eliminating it, i.e., avoiding assumptions which lead to a common and universal unit of measurement. In general, the conventional or standard way of solving the problem of psychological measurement is to make assumptions about behavior which adapt it to fit a preferred mathematical model. The new type of approach is characterized by the effort to build a mathematical model which will satisfy observed behavior.

In the approach to the general problem of psychological scaling contained in this paper there were certain fundamental issues which had to be resolved. Some of these were: what is a psychological trait in the mathematical sense, how does one recognize its presence, and how does one tell whether an attribute observed in one individual is the same attribute in another individual? An attempt to resolve these problems is contained in the chapters which follow, but a few words of orientation will be helpful. What has been done is to construct two parallel systems—a genotypic system and a phenotypic system. The genotypic system refers to an inferred, hypothetical, latent, underlying basis of behavior. The phenotypic is the manifest, the observed level of behavior. For example, a genotypic scale value would correspond to a measure of one of an individual's underlying abilities, whereas his performance on a test of that ability would represent phenotypic behavior. Thus, an individual's score on the test, as a phenotypic scale value, may be a function of the distribution of the genotypic scale values of the stimuli and could vary from one test to another with a different distribution of the genotypic scale values of the stimuli, whereas his real ability, as a genotypic scale value, may remain unchanged. What has been done is to build a strong system genotypically, a ratio scale, and a very weak system phenotypically.

A reason for using a weak phenotypic system is the fact that the information contained in a set of data is information put into those data by the underlying theory (sometimes implicit and unrecognized) in terms of which the data are analyzed. Hence, to get a great deal of information out of data, one is naturally inclined to attack it with a strong postulational system, which usually results in using numbers and the operations of arithmetic. In such instances, when one finds the data in conflict with the postulational system it is customary that the data suffer and not the measurement theory. Hence, there arises a powerful system, called error theory, random variation, and such like, to accommodate those aspects of the data incompatible with the measurement theory,

In the theory developed in this paper the postulational system defining the information contained in the observations of behavior is weak, implying that the information in the data is very crude. This position was taken from the conviction that only postulates of that level are satisfied by the types of observations of behavior made by present experimental techniques. We may observe individuals to pass or fail items in a mental test—not how well they pass or how badly they fail. We may observe individuals to indorse some statements of opinion

8

and not others, and in some methods of collecting data we may observe the order in which an individual prefers to indorse the items, and this gives us additional information. We still do not observe how strong the indorsements are in an absolute sense, but the observation does contain information on the relative magnitudes of the indorsements. *The ultimate objective of this system is to study the information contained in a set of phenotypic observations to determine what can be inferred about the genotypic level.* The point of view here is that the integrity of the data will be maintained and the level of measurement adapted to the information in the data.

A consequence of the weak system of postulates for the phenotypic level is that the theory has generality at the cost of being maximally powerful within each specific area. For this reason some of the measurement characteristics of psychophysics, mental testing, attitude measurement, interview and questionnaire procedures, essay examinations, and projective techniques can be unified. This will be the subject of a later paper.

The problems of integration and comparability of experimental studies in the same area and in different areas are first dependent upon the reduction of the methods of collecting data and the methods of analyzing data to a common unified theory.

There may well be certain areas of measurement, as, for example, certain parts of mental testing, where a stronger postulational system than this one may be satisfied. In such cases the system can be made more powerful for the description and analysis of that class of data. One way to build a stronger system is to add those postulates which are necessary for a common and constant unit of psychological measurement on the phenotypic level for each attribute. Such a system has consequences of tremendous practical value because of the variety of mathematical and statistical models available for the description and analysis of such data. In the absence of evidence for the general validity of such postulates they have not been included in this theory. To impose stronger systems in spite of data is to build an actuarial science at the possible cost of a science of individual behavior.

In the development of this theory, certain definitions and postulates about the genotypic level of behavior and certain additional postulates which link this genotypic level to the level of manifest behavior, the phenotypic level will be made explicit. In this development all the assumptions of which the writer is aware will be made explicit. The

9

basic point of view that will be taken here is that what is observed as the manifest behavior of an individual is a function of a quantitative relation between certain genotypic characteristics of the individual and the stimulus situation. From the kind of information postulated as contained in the method used for collecting data on the phenotypic level, there may be derived from the postulates certain infererences about the genotypic level.

On the basis of the definitions and postulates additional concepts or parameters will be developed to characterize certain aspects of the genotypic level of behavior. Then a corresponding set of parameters for the manifest or phenotypic level of behavior and some implications will be studied.

Because of the lack of postulates in this system which lead to numerical measurement, the types of scales with which this system is concerned are the ordered metric, the ordinal, and the partially ordered scale. Unfortunately, there are no fully developed mathematical and statistical models for the description and analysis of these classes of information. It is hoped that further development of certain areas of modern abstract algebra, topology, and order statistics will provide these models. The development of a psychological theory of this character will offer an integrated set of problems and applications for the mathematician, and it is hoped this will stimulate the development of appropriate tools for description and analysis.

Chapter III

DEFINITIONS AND POSTULATES

In this section the definitions and postulates* which will form the basis of this theory of scaling will be presented. For convenience of reference, all the definitions and postulates will be listed together and discussion will follow. Statements 1, 3-6, 8, and 10 represent a first attempt to construct a quasi-formal system, and statements 2, 7, and 9 lead to a psychological realization of this abstract system. These two divisions correspond, respectively, to a calculus and an interpretation.[6] If this were a formal mathematical development, the terms "stimulus," "individual," "moment," "attribute," and "task" would be undefined. The meaning to be given to the term "task," as used here, and the natural meanings for stimulus, individual, moment, and attribute lead to the psychological realization.

Statement 1. (Definition): A psychological attribute will be represented by a hypothetical continuum, a segment of the real line, on which is located the measure of the degree of that attribute possessed at a particular moment by an individual or a stimulus.

Statement 2. (Definition): Definition of the term "task":

a) Task A is the act of an individual evaluating a group of stimuli with respect to an ideal stimulus, the attribute being either explicit or implicit.

b) Dual task A is the act of a stimulus evaluating a group of individuals with respect to an ideal individual, the attribute being either explicit or implicit.

c) Task B is the act of an individual evaluating a group of stimuli with respect to an attribute, either explicit or implicit.

d) Dual task B is the act of a stimulus evaluating a group of individuals with respect to an attribute, either explicit or implicit.

---

*I am greatly indebted to Dr. Howard Raiffa and Professor Robert M. Thrall, both of the University of Michigan, for many suggestions for formulating these statements in a quasi-formal manner.

11

Notation: $h = 1, 2, ..., t$, where t is the total number of times an individual responds to a stimulus;

$i = 1, 2, ..., N$, where N is the total number of individuals;

$j = 1, 2, ..., n$, where n is the total number of stimuli.

Statement 3. (Postulate): Q_{hij} is the measure of a stimulus, j, on some attribute for an individual, i, at the moment, h. Q_{hij} is an element of the genotypic scale and is a single-valued function of h, i, and j and also the attribute and the task, which are suppressed variables.

Statement 4. (Postulate): C_{hij} is the measure of an individual, i, on some attribute for a stimulus, j, at the moment, h. C_{hij} is an element of the genotypic scale and is a single-valued function of h, i, and j and also the attribute and the task, which are suppressed variables.

Statement 5. (Definition): An "ideal" for an individual or stimulus is the condition

$$Q_{hij} = C_{hij} .$$

Statement 6. (Definition): The observational equation*

(1) $$P_{hij} = Q_{hij} - C_{hij}$$

defines an interveni g variable, P_{hij}, which is a psychological magnitude subject to observation.

---

* An alternative to Equation (1) is

(2) $$P_{hij} = \frac{Q_{hij} - C_{hij}}{C_{hij}} ,$$

which would be undefined for $C_{hij} = O$, i.e., the attribute in question could be regarded as meaningless or nonexistent for such an individual. Equation (1) requires the additional assumption that the unit of measurement on the genotypic continuum is biophysical and hence qualitatively and quantitatively constant over different attributes. A choice between the two must ultimately be based on experiment. It is possible that each may be valid for different objectives or different attributes. Equation (1) with statements 8a and 9a was used in an early presentation of the Unfolding Technique[8] and Equation (2) with statement 7a and a shift in origin was used in an early paper on the concepts of reliability and homogeneity[9]. The content of both these papers and the present paper are not basically affected by a choice between Equations (1) and (2).

12

Statement 7.* (Psychological Postulate):

a) $P_{hij} \leqslant 0 \iff$ responses of the category yes, agree, indorse, pass, for monotone** stimuli, positively directed (task A).

b) $|P_{hij}| \leqslant \epsilon_{hij}$ responses of the category yes, agree, indorse, for nonmonotone** stimuli and for the intermediate catagory of judgment (task A).

Statement 8. (Definition):

a) For a fixed h and i relative to task A, the symbol j ·> k means

$$|P_{hij}| \leqslant |P_{hik}|$$

b) For a fixed h and i relative to task B, the symbol j > k means

$$P_{hij} \geqslant P_{hik}$$

Statement 9. (Psychological Postulate):

a) The symbol j ·> k has the psychological interpretation "stimulus j preferred to stimulus k" (task A).

b) The symbol j > k has the psychological interpretation "stimulus j has more of (some attribute) than stimulus k" (task B).

Statement 10. (Postulate):

a) In task A for a given individual, C_{hij} depends only on the attribute, h, and i. Thus, it follows that it is independent of the genotypic scale value of the stimulus j. Symbolically, this can be represented as follows:***

$$\mathop{r}_{h,j} (C_{hij}, Q_{hij}) = 0$$

b) In dual task A for a given stimulus, Q_{hij} depends only on the attribute, h, and j. Thus, it follows that it is independent of the

---

*The symbol $\iff$ means "implies and is implied by."

**The distinction between monotone and nonmonotone stimuli is necessary in the postulates. By monotone stimuli is meant stimuli for which the number of qualitatively different kinds of responses is equal to the number of segments into which the stimulus divides the continuum. A nonmonotone item sections its continuum into more segments than it has alternatives. Monotone items are 1-1 mappings of phenotypic behavior into the genotypic scale, nonmontone items are 1-many mappings. So-called "cumulative" items are a special case of monotone items.

***This notation signifies a linear product moment correlation between the values of C_{hij} and Q_{hij} over the subscripts h and j.

13

genotypic scale value of the individual, i. Symbolically, this can be represented as follows:

$$\mathop{r}_{h,i} (C_{hij} , Q_{hij}) = 0$$

c) In task B for a given individual, C_{hij} depends only on the genotypic scale value of the stimulus, j. Symbolically, this can be represented as follows:

$$\mathop{r}_{h,j} (C_{hij} , Q_{hij}) = 1$$

d) In dual task B for a given stimulus, Q_{hij} depends only on the genotypic scale value of the individual, i. Symbolically, this can be represented as follows:

$$\mathop{r}_{h,i} (C_{hij} , Q_{hij}) = 1$$

Statement 1 identifies the concept of a psychological attribute with the mathematical concept of a continuum. This plays an important role in the mathematical definition of the concept of a trait which will be developed in detail in Chapter IV.

The term "task" as defined in Statement 2 will be discussed at length because of the several meanings of the term in ordinary usage. From a completely abstract point of view, at least two fundamentally distinct kinds of tasks can be recognized. Consider an individual responding to the items in a mental test, or answering a questionnaire as to whether he agrees with the statements, or doing paired comparisons between statements of opinion as to which statement he would prefer to indorse. The essence of each of these different situations which is common to all from the point of view of measurement theory is that the individual is evaluating each stimulus or pair of stimuli *relative* to his own position or to an ideal stimulus. In responding to the items in a mental test, the individual is comparing the Q value of each stimulus on an attribute with his C value on the same attribute. If $C \geqslant Q$, then he passes the item; if not, he fails it (see Statement 7). The "ideal" item for an individual in this case is one which requires precisely as much ability to pass it as the individual possesses. Similarly, in responding to the questionnaire items or doing paired comparisons, as above, the individual comes to these stimulus situations with his own

14

C value, with his ideal, and his responses are such that they constitute an evaluation of the Q value of each stimulus in relation to the individual's C value, or ideal. In the above cases the attribute may be either implicit or explicit. An individual might be asked which of two candidates he prefers or which of two candidates he prefers on the basis of their attitude toward foreign affairs. From the point of view of the task being performed, all the above examples illustrate the same task (task A). Note that the term "task" is not associated with a kind of attribute nor with a method of collecting data, like the Method of Single Stimuli.

Consider next the individual responding, for example, to statements of opinion, brightness, or weights, and making judgments as to how pro or con a statement is, or how bright or how heavy a stimulus is. The essence of each of these activities from the point of view of measurement is that the stimuli are being evaluated with respect to an attribute. In these instances, though the individual may have a preferred position of his own on the attribute (as may be the case for statements of opinion), this fact must nevertheless be irrelevant to his judgments for the behavior to constitute task B. This will not be pursued here with an example involving implicit attributes because this will lead us astray from the primary objectives of this monograph.

The above two types of tasks illustrate the definitions of task A and task B, respectively and for each of these two basic tasks there is a dual task in which the roles of the individual and the stimulus are interchanged. For example, in the case of the mental test items above, the response of the individual to an item may be associated with the item instead of the individual, in which case the item would be regarded as evaluating an individual with respect to its (the item's) ideal (dual task A).

Statements 3 and 4 specify the notation that will be used to represent measures of stimuli and individuals, respectively, on the genotypic continuum underlying observed behavior and also to specify certain things about these measures. In particular, whenever any individual evaluates any stimulus on any attribute according to either task A or task B there is one and only one Q value and one and only one C value.

According to Statement 3, the Q value of a stimulus may be different for different individuals and for the same individual at different times. The sources of variance of a set of Q values for a stimulus and a single individual include varying attributes with respect to which the stimulus is being evaluated, varying tasks which the individual is performing, or simply changes in the stimulus itself over a period of time. It is important to note that of all the possible sources of variance of a set of Q values only three of these sources are indicated by subscripts—time, individuals, and stimuli, i.e., h, i, and j respectively. The other two sources, attributes and tasks, are not observed. In other words, one is forced to make observations over h, i, and j, and from these somehow draw conclusions about attributes and tasks. Explicitly, a given pair of Q and C values may be associated with a stimulus, an individual, and a moment, but their magnitudes are also a function of the attribute and the task, which are suppressed variables. The experimenter may try to control attribute and task with his instructions explicitly or with the stimuli implicitly. In neither case is it *known* that the control was effective. In a broad sense, this is precisely the problem with which this theory is concerned. The Q value of a stimulus is a genotypic scale value, and, by making observations of certain characteristics of the P values (Statement 6), which depend on the method of collecting data (Statements 7, 8, and 9), certain conclusions may be drawn about attributes. For this purpose certain mathematical conditions and abstract indices necessary for the existence of unidimensional traits on the genotypic continuum will be constructed in Chapter IV.

In an exactly equivalent manner to Statement 3, Statement 4 says that the scale value, C, of an individual may be different for different stimuli and for the same stimulus at different times. The sources of variance may be varying attributes with respect to which the individual is evaluating the stimuli, varying tasks which the individual is performing, or simply changes in the individual himself over time. Thus, the genotypic scale value of an individual may be one magnitude on an attribute defined by a group of arithmetic items and another magnitude on an attribute defined by a group of statements about British foreign policy. The genotypic scale value of an individual may have a certain variance if he is judging weight stimuli with respect to whether each is heavier than a golf ball (task A) and a different degree of variance if he is judging the same stimuli on the same attribute but with respect to how heavy they are (task B). And finally, all other things remaining constant, the scale value of an individual may be one magnitude at one time and another magnitude at another time, a result of such things as growth and maturation, learning and forgetting, boredom, fatigue, etc. The note above pertaining to the possible sources of variance of a set of Q values over h, i, and j holds identically for C values. In fact, because of the symmetry of Statements 3 and 4 there is a duality theorem between the Q values of stimuli and the C values of individuals. Any

16

development of one may be rewritten for the other by recognizing the duality realized by interchanging the roles of the pairs (Q, j) and (C, i).

Statements 3 and 4 have interesting psychological implications. An individual responding to a stimulus with respect to any attribute and performing any task must be "on" the continuum, i.e., have a C value, and the same must be true of the stimulus. In the case of individuals responding to mental test items or agreeing or disagreeing with statements of opinion (task A), there is an *a priori* reasonableness about requiring that both the individual and the stimulus have genotypic scale values. But these statements go further. Statement 4 requires, for example, that even when an individual is judging which of two weights is heavier or which of two statements of opinion is more anti-X, the individual must still have a C value. It is this statement in conjunction with statement 10 which will make it possible to integrate the measurement theory of psychophysics, test theory, attitude measurement, questionnaires, and projective techniques. The distinctions between these systems can be made quantitative rather than qualitative.

In accordance with Statement 5, an ideal stimulus for an individual is one such that $Q_{hij} = C_{hij}$; for a stimulus, an ideal individual is one such that $C_{hij} = Q_{hij}$; in other words, for an ideal, $P_{hij} = 0$. As an example, if there exists a statement of opinion about the church which exactly corresponds to how an individual feels about the church, the Q value of this statement on this attribute would be identical to the C value of the individual. From the point of view of the individual, the statement is an ideal stimulus; from the point of view of the stimulus, the individual is an ideal. Another way of looking at this on the basis of later postulates is that an ideal statement of opinion is that hypothetical one which an individual would indorse in preference to all others.

Statement 6 mediates between the genotypic level (Q and C values) and the level of manifest behavior or phenotypic level (P values). This definition is permissible because the Q and C values lie on a continuum, and thus the subtraction symbol is meaningful.*

In a sense, the individual's C value may be looked upon, depending on the context, as his standard of comparison, his standard of judgment, his ability, his attitude, his norm, his set, or his point of view. Statement 6 permits each individual to have his own standard of judgment

---

*The implication of substituting Equation (2) for Equation (1) in Statement 6 is that the individual's genotypic scale value, C_{hij}, is being used as his unit of measurement.

in evaluating or responding to a stimulus; thus it may be different for the same individual for evaluating different stimuli, and it may be different for the same individual, evaluating the same stimulus, but at different times. This problem then becomes a question of experimental fact and not a matter of assumption.

In an abstract sense, P is a function of, among other things, two variables, i and j, corresponding to individuals and stimuli, respectively. The behavior of an individual in response to a stimulus may be associated with the individual or with the stimulus. In this abstract sense, stimuli and individuals are analogous. Hence any development of P from the point of view of one of these variables corresponds to an analogous development in which the roles of the two variables are interchanged. This duality of P with respect to i and j will be called the Analogy Principle.

The phrase "observational equation" is used advisedly in Statement 6 with reference to Equation (1). In a psychological measurement problem it is Q values and/or C values in which the experimenter is usually interested, but it is not these magnitudes which are observed. Rather, there is an intervening variable, P_{hij}, as given by Statement 6, and it is these P values which the experimenter actually observes. Furthermore, these P values are not usually measured in a numerical sense, but instead some degree of order relation or categorical relation among them is obtained, depending on the method of collecting data. The problem with which this theory is concerned may be described as follows: P_{hij} corresponds to the level of manifest behavior, and from the information about the P_{hij} obtained experimentally it is desired to determine precisely what can be inferred about the genotypic structure on the basis of a postulational system in which nothing will be postulated for which necessary conditions can be derived from a weaker postulational base. Thus, for a mental test as conventionally administered by the Method of Single Stimuli, the items will be thrown into two piles for each individual. One pile contains the items for which $P_{hij} \leq 0$ (the items that were passed) and the other pile contains the items that were failed, for which $P_{hij} > 0$. One knows nothing from the responses of an individual about the order of magnitude of the P values of the stimuli in the same pile. To infer this order of magnitude one may postulate that the behavior of other individuals on the test provides additional information on the basis of which inferences may be drawn about the relative magnitude of the difficulty of the items and hence the order of the P values for any one individual. This postulate is not necessary and in fact may lead to inferences incompatible with the data. Instead, from the present

18

set of postulates, the *necessary conditions* may be derived to permit such inferences from the data.

In another domain, such as an attitude continuum, one might collect data by the Method of Rank Order, asking each individual to rank the the statements in the order in which he would prefer to indorse them. It is apparent that there is another kind of information in such data. The order of magnitude of the P values of the stimuli from an ideal statement is given, but here one does not know the direction (*pro* or *con*) of the statements from the ideal statement. Other methods of collecting data contain other kinds and levels of information.

Statements 7, 8, and 9, next to be discussed, pertain to the kind and level of information contained in the observations. Statements 7 and 9 are called psychological postulates because they are of a different character from the other statements in the sense that they bridge or connect the abstract model and the psychological realization. Statement 7a expresses the necessary and sufficient condition that an individual in responding, for example, to a mental test item, will pass it if he has as much or more of that ability than is required to pass the item, and if he has less he will fail it.* This is equivalent to defining the information contained in the recorded observations of the behavior of an individual on a mental test. In the case of the monotone type of questionnaire item, administered by the Method of Single Stimuli, the individual will indorse all items up to a certain point and not beyond. An approximate example of this type of item is the questionnaire of psychophysiological correlates of fear developed by Janis *et al.*[16]

Statement 7b is necessary for the analysis and interpretation of data collected by the Method of Single Stimuli using nonmonotone items. It will take us too far afield in this monograph to develop and discuss this properly and so it will be left for a later detailed study of the Method of Single Stimuli.

Statements 8a and 9a together describe the information contained in observations on the behavior of an individual in a choice situation, such as the task of choosing which of two statements of opinion he would prefer to indorse (task A).** The quantity $|P_{hij}|$ in the language

---

*This is not the objective-type item with one right alternative and a number of wrong alternatives which an individual might "pass" by guessing.

**Statement 8 has been explicitly written for 2 categories of judgment. If an intermediate category of judgment were permitted, such as, "I don't know" this Statement would have to be modified to indicate that the expression on the left must differ from the expression on the right by at least some magnitude, such as ϵ_{hij}, in the direction indicated.

of the economist may be interpreted as a measure of utility. This will have a bearing on the interpretation of a Group scale, discussed in Chapter VIII.

Statements 8a and 9a say that an individual would prefer that stimulus whose Q value was relatively nearer his own scale position or C value. These statements are reminiscent of an equivalent type of thinking found in Horst's rationale for a zero point or indifference point for a continuum of pleasantness-unpleasantness.[15] Distance on a psychological continuum is associated with the magnitude of a psychological experience in both Horst's approach and this one. His method of collecting data, however, contains information equivalent to that contained in Statements 8a and 9a.*

Another type of choice situation used experimentally by psychologists is to secure judgments as to which of two stimuli has more of some given attribute. The type of information defined to be contained in this class of observations (task B) is given by Statement 8b and 9b together. These statements are essentially equivalent to the postulate underlying Thurstone's Law of Comparative Judgment applied to the scaling of statements of opinion or other stimuli under task B. It might be pointed out here that the Law of Comparative Judgment applied to the scaling of stimuli in which the judgments are *preferences* involves task A and hence Statements 8a and 9a rather than 8b and 9b. The implications are that there are really two Laws of Comparative Judgment which should have certain mathematical relations which can be tested experimentally. This is the subject of Chapter VIII.

There is a "theory of data"** which helps one to interrelate and understand a number of the more formal statements. The information contained in the various methods of collecting data may be organized into a four-fold table. In the first place all methods of collecting data may be divided into two general classes on the basis of the kind of task the individual is performing, task A or task B. In addition, all methods of collecting data may be divided into two general classes on the basis of the kind of behavior involved. These two classes of behavior will be called relative and irrelative. Relative behavior is

---

*In the notation of this paper, the postulate for the Method of Balanced Values would be: $P_{hij} + P_{hik} \geq 0 \Longleftrightarrow$ responses of the category yes, accept both, where P is defined by equation (1) and C is at the point of indifference. The judgment of the individual contains the information as to which P has the smaller absolute value.

**Cf. also Ref. 11.

20

behavior involving choice between two or more stimuli, e.g., which candidate do you prefer (task A) or which candidate is more x (task B). Irrelative behavior, obviously, refers to behavior involving a single stimulus at a time, e.g., will you indorse this statement (task A), can you work this arithmetic problem (task A), how do you rate x as a teacher (task B).

In general, observation of relative behavior requires use of the Method of Choice (which includes such methods as the Method of Rank Order, the Method of Paired Comparisons, and the Method of Triads); observation of irrelative behavior requires use of the Method of Single Stimuli (such as is found in many mental tests, questionnaires, and rating scales).

In the Method of Choice the data do not provide information as to whether an individual will or will not, in an absolute sense, indorse a statement. Rather, it is always information as to which of two items, say, the individual would prefer to indorse (which of the two items is psychologically nearer his own position.) In actuality, of course, the individual may detest both items or be quite willing to indorse them both, but this information is not contained in data collected by the Method of Choice. This latter "absolute" kind of information is contained in data collected by the Method of Single Stimuli and is defined by Statement 7. Thus, methods of collecting data have been classified into a four-fold table on the basis of whether they involve irrelative or relative behavior and as to whether they involve task A or task B. Statement 7 pertains exclusively to the Method of Single Stimuli, observing what is also called irrelative behavior, and Statements 8 and 9 pertain to the Method of Choice, or relative behavior. One would then expect that each of these statements would have two substatements, one for task A and one for task B. This is seen to be true of Statements 8 and 9 but not for Statement 7. Statement 7 has no substatement for task B but has *two* substatements for task A. Two substatements are needed for task A under Statement 7 because it is necessary, in this instance, to distinguish between the two kinds of stimuli, monotone and nonmonotone. Either of these kinds of stimuli may be used to collect data by the Method of Single Stimuli, task A, and there is different information contained in the data from the two kinds of stimuli. Hence different systems of analysis must be applied to the data. These distinctions will be developed in detail in a future article.

There is still, however, at least one substatement which can be added. That is a substatement 7c, for the Method of Single Stimuli,

21

task B. Substatement 7c would define the information contained in judgments of the absolute magnitudes of stimuli with respect to some attribute, and this will be immediately recognized as a method of collecting data characteristic of many rating scales. This substatement has been omitted because it is implicit in the others.

Let us summarize and illustrate Statements 7, 8, and 9. Statement 7 pertains to irrelative behavior (Method of Single Stimuli). The substatements of 7 are for task A only, one for monotone and one for nonmonotone stimuli. Substatement 7c may still have to be added. Examples of substatements 7a and 7b, respectively, are seen in the behavior of an individual in taking an arithmetic test and in taking an attitude scale, i.e., indicating whether he will indorse or not indorse each of the statements of opinion. Statements 8 and 9 pertain to choice behavior, and the substatements are for task A and task B, respectively. Statements 8a and 9a, and, Statements 8b and 9b, respectively, are represented by the behavior of an individual in judging which of two statements of opinion he would prefer to indorse and which of two statements of opinion is more anti-X.

Aside from the question of the acceptability of the statements already contained in this theory there may be independent statements which can be added, and this theory is to be regarded as by no means complete. There is no assurance that this classification of methods of collecting data is exhaustive and always adequate. Even if this classification were exhaustive now, there may still be developed new experimental methods for collecting data containing a different kind of information and hence requiring new statements to define the information.

The implications and purpose of Statement 10 will be developed in a later paper. This statement plays a role in the organization and inintegration of the domain of psychological measurement from psychophysics to projective techniques and is also relevant to the mathematical definition of a trait to be developed in Chapter IV. At this point, for the purpose of clarifying the meaning of Statement 10, its relation to Statements 3 and 4 will be pointed out. It will be recalled from previous discussion that both the individual and the stimulus always have a Q and C value when the individual responds to a stimulus. In the case of taking an arithmetic test, the individual's underlying genotypic ability, his C value, is statistically independent of the Q value of any particular item he is attempting to pass. This also pertains to an individual taking an attitude test or scale so long as the task is task A.

Consider now the case of an individual judging the felt-heaviness

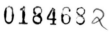

of a weight, the length of a line, or the pitch of a tone (task B). Here the individual has no C value to which he adheres, and yet by Statement 4 he must acquire one before he can make a judgment. Statement 10 says that under these circumstances, the individual takes C values correlated perfectly with the Q values of the stimuli he evaluates. The correlation of *one* may be regarded as a limiting value achieved only when the stimuli are discriminable. In the ordinary psychophysical study of j.n.d.'s, for example, this index, while it may be very high, is not *one*.

It is desirable here to clarify the notation of Statement 10. The quantity $\underset{h,j}{r}\ (C_{hij},\ Q_{hij}) = 0$, identifying task A, is a correlation coefficient associated with an individual. It is the correlation between an individual's C values and the Q values of a number of stimuli as he evaluates or responds to them; it is a correlation for a fixed i over h and j. That this coefficient has the limiting value zero for task A is simply to say that the genotypic scale values which an individual takes in responding to the group of stimuli are independent of the genotypic scale values of the stimuli. Thus, the underlying ability that an individual has is not a function of the difficulty of the item he is responding to at the moment. His *score*, of course, will reflect the difficulty of the item as well as his real ability, but his real ability is independent of the amount of the ability required to pass any particular item he is responding to.

Task B, on the other hand, is postulated to correspond to $\underset{h,j}{r}\ (C_{hij},\ Q_{hij}) = 1$. This says that the genotypic scale values of an individual in evaluating a number of stimuli with respect to an attribute will have the limiting value of perfect correlation with the genotypic scale values of the stimuli. Thus, an individual in a typical psychological experiment in judging the brightness or felt-heaviness of the stimuli has no ideal brightness or ideal weight but rather takes on a C value related to the Q value of the stimulus he is evaluating.

It would be possible to build separate systems for task A and for task B. The system for task A would be essentially the present system and the system for task B would be without C values. The reasons for not building distinct systems are two-fold. In the first place, by means of Statement 10, it will be possible to integrate into a single system the measurement problems of psychophysics, test theory and attitude scaling, questionnaires and interviews, and projective instruments. In the second place, the postulate appears intuitively to be psychologically realistic,

23

and there is experimental evidence to support it. It is interesting to reinterpret some of the experimental literature from this point of view, as, for example, the literature on anchoring experiments and factors affecting scales of judgment.

In later chapters certain implications of these statements will be developed, particularly with respect to a new experimental technique and a reinterpretation of the Law of Comparative Judgment. These will be illustrated with experiments. In Chapters IV to VI another direction of application of the theory will be developed. In Chapter IV the parameters will be developed which will be used to characterize the genotypic level, then in Chapter V the same will be done for the phenotypic level. Chapter VI will constitute an initial study of some of the relations between the genotypic and phenotypic levels implied by Statement 6. This will provide the basis for interpreting what is observed on the behavioral level in terms of its significance and implications for the genotypic level. In Chapter VII a new experimental technique deriving from the statements will be extended beyond an earlier publication[8], and in Chapter VIII the two Laws of Comparative Judgment will be developed and the relation of one of these to the Unfolding Technique will be derived and demonstrated experimentally.

Chapter IV

GENOTYPIC PARAMETERS

The quasi-formal basis for the development of a general theory of scaling has now been presented. There are many implications and consequences to be studied, some of which will be contained in this monograph. In an earlier chapter it was pointed out that this theory defines mathematically the information contained in phenotypic behavior, and hence one can study the implications and significance for the genotypic level of behavior. Before this can be done however, concepts which one is interested in on the genotypic level must be defined mathematically in order to be studied rigorously. There are, perhaps, many such concepts to be defined and there are potentially many ways of defining each. What will be done here is to define certain concepts in terms of the components of the variance of C's and Q's and these will constitute the genotypic parameters.

Psychologists are naturally more in the habit of thinking in terms of the characteristics of an individual as exhibited in his responses to a set of stimuli rather than in terms of the characteristics of a stimulus as exhibited in a set of responses from a number of individuals. Consequently, the genotypic parameters will be developed and interpreted for individuals; then by the duality theorem a corresponding set of parameters and interpretations for the stimuli will be generated. These two sets of parameters taken together will characterize the genotypic level in certain respects of interest to psychologists, but of course they are by no means to be taken as exhaustive of genotypic concepts or even the best mathematical definitions of the concepts chosen.

When an individual evaluates or responds to a number of stimuli it is necessary, from Statements 3 and 4, that he and the stimulus have a C and Q value, respectively, for each response. The variance of the distribution of all the C values of an individual for a group of stimuli will be broken down into certain selected components. These components will be identified with corresponding concepts of interest in the characterization of the behavior of the individual on the genotypic level. A decision to be faced is to choose the components of this variance. A

25

number of possibilities are open for the choice of components into which the variance is to be divided. The problem is to choose those which are of psychological significance and value. It is at this point that the question* must be faced: When is a psychological trait unidimensional?

Anastasi, in trying to find the highest common denominator for a variety of definitions, arrives at the following: "Reduced to its most elementary terms, a trait may be regarded as a category for the orderly description of the behavior of individuals" (Ref. 1, p. 127). Such a definition, while satisfying conversational requirements, does not lend itself to a mathematical translation. A better definition of an attribute for this purpose is to be found in the significant article of Bergmann and Spence: *"An attribute is not a property of physical events or objects, but is defined by means of the discriminatory responses to such objects or events on the part of observers who are different from the scientist* (original italics).... The customary definitions of attributes are all based upon the verbal discriminations of human observers or, what amounts to the same, upon their motor responses in accordance with verbal instructions. *Attributes such as pitch and loudness are thus actually defined by the consistent use of one and the same adjective and its comparative forms."* (italics not in the original) (Ref. 5, p. 14). The use of the term "consistent" in this definition provides the basis for a mathematical definition of a trait. Furthermore, inasmuch as there may be degrees of consistency, it follows that there may be degrees of an attribute. Thus, an attribute may exist to a given degree in an individual as evidenced by the degree of consistency with which *he* uses the adjective over a set of stimuli, and the attribute may be considered from the point of view of the degree to which it exists as a common attribute over a set of stimuli for a group of individuals as evidenced by the consistency in the use of the adjective *among* the individuals. These concepts of the degree of existence of an attribute within and between individuals will be merged with the concepts of the

---

* This question has importance only because of conventional modes of thought. When psychologists speak of an attribute or trait such as aggressiveness or rigidity the thinking associated with the concept almost invariably seems implicitly to assume unidimensionality. Thus, the concept of rigidity as a trait is frowned upon because some fifteen or twenty instruments presumed to measure the trait are only moderately correlated. This does not invalidate the concept but rather the notion of its unidimensionality. Rigidity may repre-present a subspace of more than one dimension within which individuals are

26

homogeneity of a set of stimuli within an individual and among a number of individuals.

A unidimensional attribute or trait can be identified with the concept of a continuum (Statement 1). A continuum is an aspect of the abstract system, and the realization of the continuum is an attribute or trait. Therefore, in testing the scalability of a set of responses of a group of individuals to a group of stimuli, one is testing the degree to which a unidimensional continuum will represent all the responses. The degree to which this is possible is then an estimate of the degree to which that behavior represents a common, organized, integrated trait for those individuals over those stimuli. To pursue the interpretation a little further, the degree of scalability is an indication of the uniformity and homogeneity of those forces (biological and/or environmental) impinging on the individuals relevant to the creation of this attribute.[2, 7] Thus, the characteristics of a society or culture are reflected in the trait organization and structure of its members. Social forces are visible only through their effects on the individual.

A very fundamental point must now be discussed. Granting the basis for the definition of an attribute quoted from Bergmann and Spence above, the question arises whether the term consistency should be applied to the behavior of an individual on the phenotypic, manifest, continuum or to the behavior of an individual on the underlying genotypic continuum. In an early attempt[9] the definitions were formulated in terms of phenotypic behavior, but the author has since become convinced that this is in error and that the definitions should pertain to the genotypic continuum. It has been found, for example, that there are conditions, although unusual ones, for which phenotypic behavior may be inconsistent when from the point of view of the genotypic continuum the attribute is a perfect trait (see Chapter VI). In fact, for a given set of genotypic parameters, for stimuli and individuals, quite a variety of phenotypic phenomena may be obtained depending on such things as the spread of stimulus differences on the genotypic continuum. Or even for a fixed

---

only partially ordered. It may be said for some pairs of individuals that one is more rigid than the other, but for some pairs of individuals this statement cannot be made—their "rigidities" are qualitatively different. To insist that all pairs of individuals be comparable in rigidity requires that they can all be projected on a unidimensional continuum in this multidimensional space in such a fashion as to preserve all initially existing order relations. This, in turn, requires that the components of rigidity be exchangeable or transmutable or compensatory.[11]

27

set of genotypic parameters, one might get very different degrees of consistency phenotypically, depending on the method of collecting data. Various methods of collecting data correspond to different powers of a microscope, and phenotypic variability may look large or small depending on the method of collecting data. This subject will be pursued in a later article and is merely mentioned here to suggest part of the basis for defining concepts genotypically rather than phenotypically. In general, the point of view taken in this paper is that concepts must be given mathematical expression on the genotypic level and that the phenotypic level then contains the indices which are constructed to represent or "measure" the concepts. These indices are frequently called empirical concepts until a theory is built which makes them part of a larger system.

Before formulating the concept of a trait in mathematical form within this theory of scaling, some general introductory remarks will be made which will clarify the reasons for the later selection of components. First, suppose that it were possible to observe the magnitude of a number of C values of an individual in responding to a set of stimuli, and that such observations had been made. For example, suppose that over a number of mental test items an individual's underlying ability, his C value, had been observed and measured for each stimulus. Suppose further, then, that such observations were to the effect that the individual had the same degree of underlying ability for all the items, i.e., that he had one and only one C value for all stimuli. If such an observation had been made, the conclusion could be drawn that these items were all measuring the same trait, e.g., arithmetic ability, on the assumption of intra-individual trait differences. Such behavior of an individual on the genotypic continuum, the complete lack of variability of his scale position (C value) over a set of stimuli, will be an example of a *perfect* trait, i.e., that each item is measuring the same (qualitative) attribute in this individual.

Suppose further that these observations had been made for a number of individuals and that each individual had one and only one C value for all the items, though, of course, different individuals may have different C values. Then the same conclusion as above could be drawn here: for each individual all the items were measuring one and the same trait. There is in this, however, no basis for the conclusion that this perfect trait behavior *within* each individual is the same trait (qualitatively) for the different individuals. This statement may appear to be making mountains out of molehills. Certainly, when the students in a

28

class are given an arithmetic test, the teacher little questions that the attribute being measured is probably arithmetic ability and certainly the same for the different individuals. This may well be, but suppose the stimuli had been a variety of situations calling for courage or bravery. And suppose further that it had been possible to observe that each individual had displayed precisely one and only one degree of this attribute over all the stimuli. Again, the conclusion could be drawn that each individual had a trait of courage or bravery which was *qualitatively* constant over these stimulus situations. But could it be said to be qualitatively the same between individuals? Is it known that the trait is not moral courage in one individual, perhaps, and physical courage in another? The answer is obviously *no.* This problem is closely related to the prevailing fallacious conviction that if a test has reliability it is measuring something. It is only necessary that it be measuring some things in each individual and not that these be the same things for the different individuals. To stray a little further for a moment, it is precisely this same assumption, on even more tenuous grounds, that underlies the use of rating scales. Where, then, can one find evidence as to whether or not these traits are the same *between* individuals? At this point it is necessary to turn to the behavior of the stimuli on the genotypic continuum.

Suppose that in the above set of hypothetical observations of the C values it had also been possible to observe the Q values of each stimulus for each individual and that the variability of the Q values of each stimulus over the individuals had been zero. Then the conclusion could be drawn that each stimulus was measuring the same trait in all individuals on the assumption, dual to the one above, of intra-stimulus trait differences. However, the conclusion could not be drawn from these observations that this perfect trait within each stimulus is the same trait (qualitatively) for the different stimuli. But now, the fact that the variability of each individual over the stimuli *and* the variability of each stimulus over the individuals had, in the same data, been observed to be zero is sufficient to demonstrate that the trait being measured is the same trait for all stimuli and individuals and would lead to the conclusion that here is a perfect trait.

These are the same circumstances which in an earlier paper were labelled class 1[8] and which would lead to a Guttman scalogram. However, are these the only circumstances, the only kind of behavior on the genotypic level, which could be classified as perfect trait behavior? The answer is *no.*

The example just discussed has involved task A. To generalize these ideas on the mathematical characteristics of a perfect trait, a hypothetical example involving task B will be given.

Suppose that the stimuli are weights of 1, 2, 4, 8, and 16 pounds and let these be labelled A, B, C, D, and E, respectively. The instructions to the subjects are to do paired comparisons as to which is heavier (task B). Let us assume that the judgments of any individual will be transitive and could be represented by the rank order I scale A B C D E.[8]

If the Unfolding Technique[8] were applied, a J scale would be generated with the stimuli ordered from light to heavy, left to right, in the order A B C D E and *all* the individuals would appear to be on this J scale to the left of the midpoint between stimuli A and B. But introspectively this is not psychologically satisfying. An individual, in judging which of two weights is heavier, does not take a position at one end of the continuum by the lightest weight which he *will* be asked about (or by the heaviest weight, either). In approaching this set of weights the individual may be considered as having no scale position of "his own" on a continuum of felt-heaviness but rather takes a scale position related to the Q value of the stimulus he is judging (Statements 2c and 10c). Thus, for task B the individual is conceived as possessing a variety of scale positions, even on the same attribute, in the course of evaluating a number of different stimuli. If then, as in the previous example it had been possible to observe the magnitudes of the C values of each individual in responding to each stimulus, they would be seen to vary from one end of the continuum to another, a relatively large variance.

Suppose, that simultaneously, as in the previous example, the Q values of each stimulus had been observed and that the variability of these genotypic scale values of each stimulus over the individuals had been zero. Here, then, would be an example of what would be a perfect trait from the point of view of each stimulus but not from the point of view of the individual if the criterion of the previous example were applied. The problem, then, is to construct a mathematical definition of the concept of a perfect trait such that *both* the previous example of task A and this example of task B would satisfy it. This is not difficult to do. What characterizes the variability of the C values of an individual in this instance is its *regularity* in relation to the Q values of the stimuli being judged. Under these circumstances, if one takes out of the total variance of the C values of an individual so much of it as is accountable for by relation to the variability of the Q values of the stimuli, no variance remains, in this hypothetical example,

30

and the behavior may again be classified as a perfect trait.

This principle of "regularity" of behavior on the genotypic continuum will be the basic principle for defining what is meant by a trait. The question is: Can an individual have different C values on the same attribute in successively evaluating a number of stimuli over an interval of time? This question in the case of a perfect trait is answered *no* for task A, *yes* for task B.

One further consideration must now be added before proceeding to the mathematical formulation of these ideas. Up to this point only the variance of an individual's C values which can be accounted for by the nature of the task set by the experimenter has entered into the definition of a perfect trait. But this principle of regularity has more general applicability than just to the distinction between tasks. There may be variance of an individual's C values, under either task A or task B, due to some other experimentally controlled agent than just the task set. In particular, it will be proper to remove from the total variance of an individual's C values such components as are attributable to any other experimental variable. In a more general sense, there may be variance of the C values attributable to learning or forgetting over the period of observation, or experimental administration of drugs, or propaganda, or some other predictable or controlled source acting over time. Only so much of the total variance of the C values of an individual in responding repeatedly to a number of stimuli that is not accountable for will be cause to distrust the interpretation that the behavior represents a perfect trait. This unaccounted-for variance is what constitutes what is called random error variance in statistical theories of measurement. This leaves the implication that less than complete identity among the attributes underlying the behavior constitutes a source of this so-called random error variance. It should be noted that the preceding arguments, while all from the point of view of the variance of C values, may be dualistically repeated for the variance of Q values. Hence the mathematical development of the concept of a trait will utilize both of these points of view.

Consider an individual who is a member of a group of individuals each of whom has responded to each of a set of stimuli a number of times. It makes no difference for these purposes whether the stimuli were a set of ink blots or the items in a mental test; it makes no difference whether the same attribute was the basis for all of the judgments or not; and it does not matter how the individual interpreted the instructions of the experimenter or examiner. It is

31

sufficient that there be a number of C values for each individual. The scale value of the individual on the genotypic level is defined to be the mean of all his C values, thus:

$$(3) \qquad C_{.i.} = \frac{1}{nt} \sum_j \sum_h C_{hij}$$

Also of interest is the variability of the individual's C values and, in particular, the sources from which it arises. It was observed that an individual may have different C values for a variety of reasons, and it is necessary to break this variance down into some of its components which would have psychological significance. It is apparent from the previous discussion of the concept of a psychological trait that the components of the variance of an individual's behavior on the genotypic level that will be of significance are the within-stimuli and between-stimuli components, with certain modifications. These parameters will now be developed.

The total variance of an individual's C values will be designated $v_{.i.}$ and is given by:

$$(4) \qquad v_{.i.} = \frac{1}{nt} \sum_j \sum_h (C_{hij} - C_{.i.})^2 \ .$$

Defining:

$$(5) \qquad C_{.ij} = \frac{1}{t} \sum_h C_{hij} \ ,$$

$$(6) \qquad C_{..j} = \frac{1}{Nt} \sum_i \sum_h C_{hij} \ , \text{ and}$$

$$(7) \qquad C_{...} = \frac{1}{Nnt} \sum_i \sum_j \sum_h C_{hij} \ ,$$

the total variance may be broken down into its within- and between-stimuli components by the usual analysis of variance technique:

$$(8) \qquad v_{.i.} = d_{.i.}^2 + \sigma^2_{j\,C_{.ij}} \ ,$$

where

$$(9) \qquad d_{.i.}^2 = \frac{1}{nt} \sum_j \sum_h (C_{hij} - C_{.ij})^2 \ ,$$

32

(10)
$$\sigma^2_{j C_{\cdot ij}} = \frac{1}{n} \sum_j (C_{\cdot ij} - C_{\cdot i \cdot})^2 .$$

From the variance between stimuli, $\sigma^2_{j C_{\cdot ij}}$, so much of it as is attributable to agents varying in a controlled and known manner during the experiment must be removed. This component of the variance is determined by the multiple, nonlinear regression of $C_{\cdot ij}$ on such agents. Representing by $t^2_{\cdot i \cdot}$ the variance of an individual between stimuli not attributable to the controlled variation of other agents, we can write:

(11)
$$t^2_{\cdot i \cdot} = \sigma^2_{j C_{\cdot ij}} (1 - \eta^2_{j C_{\cdot ij}.12 \cdots a}) ,$$

where a is the number of known controlled agents generating variance of $C_{\cdot ij}$ over $j \cdot$. This quantity, $t^2_{\cdot i \cdot}$, will be fundamental to the quantitative definition of a trait.

Substituting Equation (11) in (8), the total variance of an individual's C_{hij} values over a group of stimuli becomes:

(12)
$$v_{\cdot i \cdot} = d^2_{\cdot i \cdot} + t^2_{\cdot i \cdot} + \eta^2_{j C_{\cdot ij}.12 \cdots a} \sigma^2_{j C_{\cdot ij}}$$

Equation (12) is in some respects a more general case than is required for most experiments involving scaling on a single continuum. Because measurement problems are classifiable on the basis of relations between Q and C values and because this relation is the most common single source of the variance of the C values of an individual over a group of stimuli, the expression for $t^2_{\cdot i \cdot}$ may be simplified by taking into account only this one source of variance. In the simpler case in which the only controlled agent contributing variance on the genotypic level to the between-stimuli component is the type of task being performed (Statement 10), Equation (12) simplifies to:

(13)
$$v_{\cdot i \cdot} = d^2_{\cdot i \cdot} + t^2_{\cdot i \cdot} + r^2_{h,j}(C_{hij} , Q_{hij}) \sigma^2_{j C_{\cdot ij}} ,$$

(14)
$$t^2_{\cdot i \cdot} = \sigma^2_{j C_{\cdot ij}} [1 - r^2_{h,j}(C_{hij} , Q_{hij})] .$$

When an experimenter asks an individual to judge stimuli with respect

33

to an attribute (task B) and the individual does so, the variance of the individual's C values has a contribution due to the fact that C_{hij} is related to Q_{hij} over h and j. This variance is not variance which should detract from the trait concept $t_{.i.}^2$, and hence is removed as indicated in Equation (14).

When an experimenter asks an individual to give his preferences between stimuli (task A), then C_{hij} and Q_{hij} are independent (Statement 10a), and $t_{.i.}$ simply comprises all the variance of the individual between stimuli.

Equations (13) and (14), as special cases of (12) and (11), respectively, will be the ones of primary interest in this monograph. It is desirable to point out that Equations (11) and (12) are not completely general, however, in that they do not include the case in which relevant agents are varied *within* stimuli.

Certain of the parameters that will be used to characterize the behavior of individuals on the genotypic level have now been developed.

The quantity $d_{.i.}^2$ defines the *concept* of the reliability of *an* individual over a set of stimuli on the genotypic level. The quantity $t_{.i.}^2$ defines the *concept* of the homogeneity of an individual over a set of stimuli on the genotypic level.

The corresponding set of parameters that characterize the behavior of the stimuli on the genotypic continuum follow readily from the duality theorem.

To preserve the duality theorem, the scale value of a stimulus on the genotypic level is defined to be

$$(15) \qquad Q_{..j} = \frac{1}{Nt} \sum_i \sum_h Q_{hij} \, ,$$

and the total variance of the Q values of a stimulus is defined to be

$$(16) \qquad v_{..j} = \frac{1}{Nt} \sum_i \sum_h (Q_{hij} - Q_{..j})^2 \, .$$

In accordance with the duality theorem, the following additional definitions are made:

$$(17) \qquad Q_{.ij} = \frac{1}{t} \sum_h Q_{hij} \, ,$$

$$(18) \qquad Q_{.i.} = \frac{1}{nt} \sum_j \sum_h Q_{hij} \, ,$$

34

(19)
$$Q... = \frac{1}{Nnt} \sum_i \sum_j \sum_h Q_{hij} \, ,$$

(20)
$$d^2_{..j} = \frac{1}{Nt} \sum_i \sum_h (Q_{hij} - Q_{.ij})^2 \, ,$$

(21)
$$\sigma^2_{i Q_{.ij}} = \frac{1}{N} \sum_i (Q_{.ij} - Q_{..j})^2 \, .$$

From the duality theorem, the general expressions for stimuli that correspond to Equations (8), (11), and (12) for individuals are:

(22)
$$v_{..j} = d^2_{..j} + \sigma^2_{i Q_{.ij}} \, ,$$

(23)
$$t^2_{..j} = \sigma^2_{i Q_{.ij}} (1 - \eta^2_{i Q_{.ij}. 12 \cdots a}) \, ,$$

(24)
$$v_{..j} = d^2_{..j} + t^2_{..j} + \eta^2_{i Q_{.ij}. 12 \cdots a} \, \sigma^2_{Q_{.ij}} \, .$$

In the special case i. which the sole controlled source of variance of Q values between individuals is the task being performed by the stimulus, Equation (24) simplifies to:

(25)
$$v_{..j} = d^2_{..j} + t^2_{..j} + r^2_{h,i}(C_{hij}, Q_{hij}) \, \sigma^2_{i Q_{.ij}} \, ,$$

where

(26)
$$t^2_{..j} = \sigma^2_{i Q_{.ij}} [1 - r^2_{h,i}(C_{hij}, Q_{hij})] \, .$$

The quantity $d^2_{..j}$ defines the *concept* of the reliability of a stimulus over a set of individuals on the genotypic level. The quantity $t^2_{..j}$ defines the *concept* of the homogeneity of a stimulus over a group of individuals on the genotypic level.

A mathematical definition of a perfect trait may now be formulated. The behavior of a group of individuals in responding to a group of stimuli constitutes a perfect trait if and only if:

35

$$(27)^* \qquad t^2_{\cdot i \cdot} - t^2_{\cdot \cdot i} = 0 \quad \text{for all } i \text{ and } j.$$

The concept of homogeneity for the genotypic behavior of a group of individuals over a set of stimuli would be defined by some function of $t^2_{\cdot i \cdot}$, for example, an average. Similarly, there would exist the concept of homogeneity of a set of stimuli over a group of individuals and would be defined by a similar function of $t^2_{\cdot \cdot j}$. Equation 27 represents an extreme case of perfect homogeneity of individuals over stimuli and stimuli over individuals.

For task A this implies that for a perfect trait there is no variation of the genotypic scale values of either stimuli or individuals. For task B this implies that for a perfect trait all the variance of the C values of individuals is attributable to their correlation with the Q values of the stimuli. One of the problems to be answered in a later chapter is what values the parameters which describe the manifest behavior on the phenotypic level will have under this condition of a perfect trait.

The investigation of the relation between genotypic and phenotypic behavior contained in this monograph is concerned exclusively with Joint scales, which may now be defined precisely by the parameters

$$(28) \qquad \mathop{r}_{h,j} (C_{hij}, Q_{hij}) = \mathop{r}_{h,i} (C_{hij}, Q_{hij}) = 0$$

for all i and j. Verbally, in a Joint scale, genotypic scale values of the individuals are independent of the genotypic scale values of stimuli, and, similarly, the genotypic scale values of stimuli are independent of the genotypic scale values of individuals.

Those parameters which will serve certain immediate purposes in describing the characteristics of the genotypic level of behavior have now been developed. In the next chapter a corresponding set of parameters for characterizing the phenotypic or observed level of behavior will be developed and then these two sets of parameters will be brought together and some of their interrelations studied under the conditions of a Joint scale.

---

*This is strictly true only if $d^2_{\cdot i \cdot}$ and $d^2_{\cdot \cdot j}$ are both zero. We are here neglecting variance between groups due to random variations.

Chapter V

PHENOTYPIC PARAMETERS

In the previous chapter those parameters were developed that characterize certain aspects of the genotypic level of behavior, i.e., the underlying, inferred, or conceptual level of behavior. According to Statements 6, 7, 8, and 9, however, these are not the characteristics of behavior which are directly observed or which are manifest in data. Rather, what is manifest in the behavior of individuals is certain information about P values. The amount and kind of information about P values is dependent upon the method of collecting data. Such procedures for collecting data as the Method of Single Stimuli, the Method of Rank Order, the Method of Paired Comparisons, and the Method of Triads contain different *amounts* and even different *kinds* of information.

It is the intent of this section to develop certain parameters to describe or characterize manifest behavior. This will be done not for any single method of collecting data, but in the abstract and independent of the method of collecting data. Any particular method of data collection may then be studied to determine what information, if any, such a method contains with respect to a particular parameter. In the next section some of the relations between the pattern of genotypic parameters and the pattern of phenotypic parameters will be studied.

As in the case of genotypic parameters there is the choice of developing the phenotypic parameters from the point of view of the behavior of individuals over a group of stimuli or from the point of view of the the behavior of stimuli over a group of individuals. As before, the choice will be to develop the parameters from the point of view of describing the manifest behavior of individuals and then, by the Analogy Principle, develop a corresponding set of parameters which will describe the manifest behavior of stimuli.

Consider an individual who is a member of a group of individuals each of whom has responded a number of times to each of a set of stimuli. For each individual, each time he responds to a stimulus, there is, in principle, a score, P_{hij}, which may be regarded as an abstract psychological value at that time for that stimulus for that individual. In the case of a mental test item, P_{hij} may be regarded as the difficulty of the item for the individual, or the score of the individual on the item.

Let the status score[7] of an individual be defined as the arithmetic mean of his scores on the items

$$(29)* \qquad P_{.i.} = \frac{1}{nt} \sum_j \sum_h P_{hij}$$

$P_{.i.}$ may be viewed as the scale value of the individual on the *manifest* phenotypic continuum in order to distinguish it from the scale value, $C_{.i.}$, of the individual on the underlying genotypic continuum. In an approximate sense, $P_{.i.}$ would correspond to the score of an individual on a test, whereas $C_{.i.}$ would represent his real ability on the underlying attribute measured by the test. From the postulates it can readily be seen that the status score of an individual, a characteristic of his manifest behavior, is a function of his real abilities and the distribution of the difficulties of the items on the underlying attributes.

It is a consequence of the postulates that various methods of collecting data provide various degrees of information about P values on the manifest continuum, and the problem is to determine from the characteristics of these P values what the characteristics of the underlying (genotypic) continuum are. The characteristics of the genotypic continuum are those described by the parameters developed in the previous chapter. In a similar manner the characteristics of the phenotypic continuum will be descriued by a set of parameters analogous to those describing the genotypic continuum.

Consider the variance of the distribution of P_{hij} for a given i . The appropriate components of this variance will constitute the parameters characterizing the manifest behavior of an individual. Again, alternative decompositions of the variance are available, and the problem is to select the one which will provide components of psychological significance. In the case of genotypic variance a version of within- and between-stimuli components was used. Here, in the case of phenotypic variance the same reasoning will be followed.

Designating by $V_{.i.}$ the total variance of the phenotypic scale values of an individual in responding to each of n stimuli, t times, gives:

$$(30) \qquad V_{.i.} = \frac{1}{nt} \sum_j \sum_h (P_{hij} - P_{.i.})^2 .$$

*The origin from which the status score is computed was defined differently in an earlier paper [9] in order to simplify the developments in that paper. The definition here is a more general one, and development of $V_{.i.}$ here contains the development of $V_{.i.}$ in that paper as a special case.

38

Defining:

$$(31) \qquad P_{.ij} = \frac{1}{t} \sum_h P_{hij} ,$$

$$(32) \qquad P_{..j} = \frac{1}{Nt} \sum_i \sum_h P_{hij} , \text{ and}$$

$$(33) \qquad P_{...} = \frac{1}{Nnt} \sum_i \sum_j \sum_h P_{hij}$$

$V_{.i.}$ can be broken into components by adding and subtracting $P_{.ij}$ inside the parentheses of Equation (30) expanding, and collecting terms.

Defining:

$$(34) \qquad D^2_{.i.} = \frac{1}{nt} \sum_j \sum_h (P_{hij} - P_{.ij})^2 ,$$

$$(35) \qquad \sigma^2_{j\,P_{.ij}} = \frac{1}{n} \sum_j (P_{.ij} - P_{.i.})^2 , \text{ and}$$

$$(36) \qquad V_{.i.} = D^2_{.i.} + \sigma^2_{j\,P_{.ij}} ,$$

the total variance of the phenotypic scale values of an individual is divided into two components, a variance within stimuli and a variance between stimuli.

As in the case of the genotypic parameters, so much of the variance between stimuli, $\sigma^2_{j\,P_{.ij}}$, as is attributable to agents varying in a controlled and known manner during the experiment will be removed. Such variance is determined by the multiple nonlinear regression of $P_{.ij}$ on such agents. Letting $T^2_{.i.}$ represent the variance of an individual between stimuli not attributable to the controlled variation of other agents, gives:

$$(37) \qquad T^2_{.i.} = \sigma^2_{j\,P_{.ij}} (1 - \eta^2_{j\,P_{.ij}.12\cdots a}) .$$

Substituting from (37) into (36), the total variance of an individual's phenotypic scale values over a group of stimuli may be written:

$$(38) \qquad V_{.i.} = D^2_{.i.} + T^2_{.i.} + \eta^2_{j\,P_{.ij}.12\cdots a} \sigma^2_{j\,P_{.ij}} .$$

39

In the simplest case in which the sole source of controlled variance of the individual between stimuli is due to the spread of scale values of the stimuli on the phenotypic level, Equation (38) simplifies to

$$(39) \qquad V_{.i.} = D^2_{.i.} + T^2_{.i.} + r^2_{P_{.ij}P_{..j}} \; \sigma^2_{j \, P_{.ij}} \; ,$$

where

$$(40) \qquad T^2_{.i.} = \sigma^2_{j \, P_{.ij}} (1 - r^2_{P_{.ij}P_{..j}}) \; .$$

There are three parameters in these equations, $D^2_{.i.}$, $T^2_{.i.}$, and $r_{P_{.ij}P_{..j}}$, which are of psychological significance, and hence their interpretation will be discussed. $D^2_{.i.}$ has been discussed in detail elsewhere[7] and that discussion will only be summarized here. In summary, $D^2_{.i.}$ represents the variance of the status score of *an* individual on a test, the precision of the score, which can be identified with a measure or *index* of reliability. It must be recognized that this is reliability from the point of view of that particular set of items comprising that test, a hypothetically experimentally independent test-retest reliability for a single individual. This index is distinct from that represented by $V_{.i.}$. The latter is the variability of a score on a test viewed as a score on the universe of items from which the sample comprising the test has been drawn. In this latter case, the score is viewed as a score on an *attribute*, and the test contains a sample of items from the domain of that attribute. Obviously, in this case the homogeneity of the domain has important bearing on the variability of an individual's score from sample to sample. This latter characteristic of the domain, its homogeneity, is related in part to the parameter $T^2_{.i.}$.

Consider, for example, a perfectly homogeneous domain in which each individual's ability is constant over all the items, $C_{hij} = C_{.i.}$ (but not necessarily the same for all individuals) and the Q value of each item is constant for all individuals $Q_{hij} = Q_{..j}$. The score $(P_{.ij})$ of each individual on each item is then invariant over repetition but will be perfectly correlated with the difficulty of the item, i.e., $r_{P_{.ij}P_{..j}} = +1$. Under these extreme and unusual conditions which serve these didactic purposes, $D_{.i.} = T_{.i.} = 0$. Thus the score on such a test is perfectly precise, the items are perfectly homogeneous, but $V_{.i.}$ is greater than zero. There is still variance of an individual's score on the *attribute* by virtue of the fact that the distribution of item difficulties would vary from sample to sample. This is the component of $V_{.j.}$, represented by the last term of Equation (39).

The parameter $r_{P_{.ij}P_{..j}}$ is a characteristic of an *individual*, as are all the terms of Equation (39). This index is the correlation between the difficulties of the items for this individual and the difficulties of the items for the group as a whole. This is an indication of how similar the attribute on which the individual is evaluating the stimuli is to the attribute for the group as a whole. Such a parameter may be interpreted as the "belongingness" of an individual to the group from a cultural point of view. This parameter is an index of the degree to which the attribute underlying these stimuli is constituted or constructed for him as it is for the group as a whole. This index is a basis for the construction of an index for the homogeneity of a group of individuals.

While interpretations of the parameters given above were cast in the context of mental testing, they may be generalized further into the domain of so-called qualitative variables. These extended interpretations will be left for a later time.

It was intended that these phenotypic parameters characterize aspects of the manifest data. These aspects may now be considered specifically. It is immediately apparent from the definition of $D_{.i.}^2$ (Equation 34) and the postulates that, if $D_{.i.}^2 = 0$, then P_{hij} is a constant over h for all j for individual i , and hence paired comparisons between the stimuli by that individual would be consistent and transitive: consistent in the sense that if any pairs of stimuli were repeated, the judgments or responses would be repeated also; transitive in the sense that the paired comparisons could be perfectly represented by an I scale[8] which would be a simple order, and the same data could have been collected by the Method of Rank Order rather than by the Method of Paired Comparisons. However, it should be noted, that if the data had been collected by the Method of Rank Order, it would not be known that $D_{.i.}^2$ would have been zero if paired comparisons had been used. $D_{.i.}^2$ is forced equal to zero if the Method of Rank Order is used instead of paired comparisons.

It should be pointed out that if the paired comparisons of an individual are transitive, suggesting $D_{.i.}^2 = 0$, this in no way implies that the judgments of the stimuli are based on a common attribute and hence constitute a well-organized integrated trait for the individual. The basis of judgment or decision is a P value, and a sufficient condition

41

for $D^2_{\cdot i\cdot} = 0$ is that each stimulus be consistently evaluated on one attribute, and it is not further necessary that it be the same attribute for all the stimuli. The parameter $T^2_{\cdot i\cdot}$ is the one which is relevant to this concept. This problem will be pursued a little further after developing the phenotypic parameters for stimuli.

From the Analogy Principle the following equations may be written:

$$(41) \qquad V_{\cdot \cdot j} = \frac{1}{Nt} \sum_i \sum_h (P_{hij} - P_{\cdot \cdot j})^2 ,$$

$$(42) \qquad D^2_{\cdot \cdot j} = \frac{1}{Nt} \sum_i \sum_h (P_{hij} - P_{\cdot ij})^2 ,$$

$$(43) \qquad \sigma^2_{i\,P_{\cdot ij}} = \frac{1}{N} \sum_i (P_{\cdot ij} - P_{\cdot \cdot j})^2 , \text{ and}$$

$$(44) \qquad V_{\cdot \cdot j} = D^2_{\cdot \cdot j} + \sigma^2_{i\,P_{\cdot ij}} .$$

Following the same reasoning as that used in developing the phenotypic parameters for individuals but this time reversing the roles of stimuli and individuals gives:

$$(45) \qquad T^2_{\cdot \cdot j} = \sigma^2_{i\,P_{\cdot ij}} (1 - \eta^2_{i\,P_{\cdot ij}.12\cdots a}) ,$$

$$(46) \qquad V_{\cdot \cdot j} = D^2_{\cdot \cdot j} + T^2_{\cdot \cdot j} + \eta^2_{i\,P_{\cdot ij}.12\cdots a}\, \sigma^2_{i\,P_{\cdot ij}}$$

In the simplest case in which the sole source of controlled variance of the phenotypic scores (difficulties) of a stimulus over individuals is the spread of abilities of the individuals on the phenotypic level, Equation (46) simplifies to

$$(47) \qquad V_{\cdot \cdot j} = D^2_{\cdot \cdot j} + T^2_{\cdot \cdot j} + r^2_{P_{\cdot ij}P_{\cdot i\cdot}}\, \sigma^2_{i\,P_{\cdot ij}} ,$$

where

$$(48) \qquad T^2_{\cdot \cdot j} = \sigma^2_{i\,P_{\cdot ij}} (1 - r^2_{P_{\cdot ij}P_{\cdot i\cdot}}) .$$

This analysis provides a set of parameters for the manifest behavior of a stimulus over a group of individuals analogous to those describing the manifest behavior of an individual over a group of stimuli. The interpretations of these parameters for a stimulus are identical to their counterparts for an individual with the roles of stimuli and individuals reversed. The quantity $D^2_{..j}$ has the identical meaning for stimuli that $D^2_{.i.}$ has for individuals, and it is evident that

$$D^2_{.i.} = 0 \iff D^2_{..j} = 0$$

as each parameter is equal to zero if and only if $P_{hij} = P_{.ij}$. It has already been indicated that the parameters $T^2_{.i.}$ and $T^2_{..j}$ are related to the concept of homogeneity. They represent respectively the unaccountable variance of the manifest behavior of an individual between stimuli and the corresponding unaccountable variance of a stimulus between people.

It is to be noted that $T^2_{.i.} = 0$ if and only if either

1) $\sigma^2_{P_{.ij}} = 0$, or

2) $r_{P_{.ij} P_{..j}} = 1.0$,

and by the Analogy Principle there is a corresponding set of conditions for $T^2_{..j}$. The complete implications of these conditions cannot be pursued in detail here, but the interpretations of the parameters $T_{.i.}$ and $T^2_{..j}$ will be briefly pointed out. In the case of Joint scales, both $T^2_{.i.}$ and $T^2_{..j}$ appear to be equal to zero when the I scales or the S scales are all members of a single set from one J scale with known metric relations. In more conventional terminology, these two quantities are equal to zero when the responses of the individuals to the stimuli can be completely described by a single underlying continuum, on which, in the case of Joint scales, both stimuli and individuals can be ordered and common metric relations are observed. Essentially, these two quantities represent measures of homogeneity of a given set of data from two different points of view. The quantity $T^2_{.i.}$ represents homogeneity from the point of view of the manifest behavior of an individual over stimuli, whereas the quantity $T^2_{..j}$ represents homogeneity from the point of view of the behavior of a stimulus over individuals.

43

As indicated previously, $r_{P_{.ij}P_{..j}}$ reflects the belongingness of an individual to a group of individuals for this group of stimuli. The analogous parameter, $r_{P_{.ij}P_{.i.}}$, is a characteristic of each stimulus and has the dual interpretation. It reflects the belongingness of a stimulus to the group of stimuli for this group of individuals.

These phenotypic indices are of assistance in gaining an understanding of the two concepts of homogeneity that·have been generated by this mathematical development. Consider the behavior of a group of individuals in response to a set of stimuli. The problems which are faced from the point of view of whether this mass of behavior represents a perfect trait, or the degree to which it does, is dependent upon two conditions; namely, (1) the degree to which the stimuli belong together from the point of view of the similarity of their behavior over a group of individuals and (2) the degree to which the individuals belong together from the point of view of the similarity of their behavior over a group of stimuli.

If traits are generated or affected by cultural or biological influences, then a set of stimuli, all pertaining to the same trait, e.g., attitude toward the negro, may not be homogeneous among themselves because the group of individuals who are responding to the stimuli are culturally or biologically heterogen·ous in the relevant aspects. And then, similarly, there is a dual concept, namely, that a group of individuals may not be homogeneous among themselves in the behavior analyzed because the stimuli are heterogeneous, e.g., there may be an arithmetic item among a lot of spelling items in a test.

These two coefficients, $r_{P_{.ij}P_{.i.}}$, and $r_{P_{.ij}P_{..j}}$ are characteristics of stimuli and individuals, respectively, and are indicative of the degree to which a stimulus "belongs" to the group of stimuli and the degree to which an individual "belongs" to the group of individuals. Lack of homogeneity may come from either source, stimuli or individuals.

It is interesting to note that the conventional mode of thought associates the concept of homogeneity with the belongingness of *stimuli* and of reliability as an indication of the numerical precision of *individual's* scores. This development suggests that each of these concepts has its dual, i.e., that the data might lack homogeneity because the *individuals* do not belong together, i.e., that there is also a matter of the reliability with which the *stimuli's* scale positions have been determined.

The parameters $T_{.i.}^2$ and $T_{..j}^2$ are more general parameters with the same significance and interpretation as the two correlation coefficients. The two correlation coefficients may themselves serve as trait scores in place of $T_{.i.}^2$ and $T_{..j}^2$ in the case of Joint scales. But the more general parameters $T_{.i.}^2$ and $T_{..j}^2$ are applicable also to other classes of scales, as, for example, psychophysical or stimulus scales. The detailed development of this will be pursued at a later time.

A set of parameters has now been developed and discussed which is descriptive of certain aspects of manifest data of interest and significance to social scientists. These parameters are all observable in the data at a crude level of approximation. Therein lies the present major weakness of social and psychological data. These hypothetical quantities, P_{hij} , *are in general not experimentally measured.* Experimentally, their measurement requires that the data indicate how *well* an individual passes an arithmetic item or how *badly* he fails a spelling item or precisely to what degree he indorses a statement. Depending upon the method by which data are collected, various degrees of information about the magnitudes of P_{hij} are obtained. Of course, a high degree of information can appear to be obtained if additional assumptions are made such as those involved in the use of a numerical rating scale. An analysis of the nature and degree of information contained in the various methods of collecting data and some of the special assumptions that are required is very fascinating and revealing but cannot be pursued in this monograph.*

Having developed a set of genotypic parameters and a set of phenotypic parameters their interrelations will now be investigated to try to discover what interpretations on a genotypic level may follow from certain observed characteristics of the phenotypic level.

---

*Cf. also Ref. 11.

Chapter VI

THE AREA OF JOINT SCALES

Certain interrelations between the genotypic and phenotypic parameters will be studied in this chapter. The problem here is what the data, when collected by a given method, look like, for various characteristics of the genotypic level. This is an immense problem. The theory developed here, however, makes possible, in principle, the theoretical analysis of such relationships. Certain segments of this problem have been studied and the results will be presented.

There are four basic genotypic parameters which span a space of four dimensions within which may be located patterns of characteristics of the phenotypic behavior. These four genotypic parameters which provide a basis for organizing the domain of scaling are the quantities $\underset{h,i}{r}(C_{hij}, Q_{hij})$, $\underset{h,j}{r}(C_{hij}, Q_{hij})$, $V_{\cdot i \cdot}$, and $V_{\cdot \cdot j}$. In the domain of of what is here called Joint scales, (e.g., attitude scales, mental tests) the correlation coefficient $\underset{h,j}{r}(C_{hij}, Q_{hij})$ is zero, indicating that the C value which an individual takes in responding to a stimulus is independent of the Q value of the stimulus. To make a concrete interpretation, if there were a number of items, all measuring the *identical* mental ability, the amount of this trait the individual possessed would *not* be dependent on the amount necessary to pass a particular item.

The index $\underset{h,i}{r}(C_{hij}, Q_{hij})$ has the dual interpretation for stimuli. This is an index of the degree to which the Q values of the stimuli are related to the C values of the individuals responding to them. In the domain of Joint scales, this coefficient is zero also. The interpretation of this is that the amount of an ability required to pass an item is not related to the amount of that ability possessed by an individual who is responding to the item. All these statements, of course, apply to scale values on an underlying genotypic continuum and not to phenotypic indices, such as numerical scores on a test.

Thus the definition of the domain of Joint scales will be the values $\underset{h,j}{r}(C_{hij}, Q_{hij}) = \underset{h,i}{r}(C_{hij}, Q_{hij}) = 0$. This surface will be referred to

46

as the (0, 0) grid. On this surface, the two remaining genotypic parameters $V_{.j.}$ and $V_{..j}$ may take values from zero to indefinitely large. Certain magnitudes will be inferred on these two genotypic parameters, and the consequent magnitude of the phenotypic parameters will be investigated. Thus the domain of Joint scales may be organized as in Figure 1.

$d_j^2 > 0, \ t_j^2 > 0$ $v_{.j} = d_j^2 + \sigma_{h,i}^2 Q_{hij}$	$(0,0)_{41}$	$(0,0)_{42}$	$(0,0)_{43}$	$(0,0)_{44}$
$d_j^2 = 0, \ t_j^2 > 0$ $v_{.j} = \sigma_{h,i}^2 Q_{hij}$	$(0,0)_{31}$	$(0,0)_{32}$	$(0,0)_{33}$	$(0,0)_{34}$
$d_j^2 > 0, \ t_{.j}^2 = 0$ $v_{.j} = d_{.j}^2$	$(0,0)_{21}$	$(0,0)_{22}$	$(0,0)_{23}$	$(0,0)_{24}$
$d_j^2 = 0, \ t_{.j}^2 = 0$ $v_{.j} = 0$	$(0,0)_{11}$	$(0,0)_{12}$	$(0,0)_{13}$	$(0,0)_{14}$
	$d_{.i}^2 = 0, \ t_{.i}^2 = 0$ $v_{.i} = 0$	$d_{.i}^2 > 0, \ t_{.i}^2 = 0$ $v_{.i} = d_{.i}^2$	$d_{.i}^2 = 0, \ t_{.i}^2 > 0$ $v_{.i} = \sigma_{h,j}^2 C_{hij}$	$d_{.i}^2 > 0, \ t_{.i}^2 > 0$ $v_{.i} = d_{.i}^2 + \sigma_{h,j}^2 C_{hij}$

Figure 1.

The lower left-hand corner of Figure 1 is regarded as the origin, and rows and columns are counted from it. The grid results from an arbitrary segmentalizing of the two continuous coordinate axes. This is done merely to permit algebraic study and to provide a simple classification system for the surface. The phenotypic parameters characterizing the hypothetical manifest data which would be associated with a designated cell will be calculated.

The simplest case, the class $(0, 0)_{11}$ will be considered first. For this class, as may be seen in Figure 1, the genotypic parameters have the following conditions:

$$d_{..j}^2 = 0 \ , \ t_{..j}^2 = 0 \ , \ d_{.i.}^2 = 0 \ , \ t_{.i.}^2 = 0$$

It immediately follows from the equations defining these parameters, i.e., Equations (20), (26), (9), and (14), that

$$Q_{hij} = Q_{..j} \ , \ C_{hij} = C_{.i.}$$

47

This is merely to say that each stimulus had one and only one genotypic scale value for all individuals every time they responded to it, and each individual had one and only one genotypic scale value regardless of which stimulus he responded to or when he responded.

From the postulates and Equations (1), (31), (32), (29), and (33), the following quantities may be written:

$$(49) \qquad P_{hij} = P_{.ij} = Q_{..j} - C_{.i.} \, ,$$

$$(50) \qquad P_{..j} = Q_{..j} - C_{...} \, ,$$

$$(51) \qquad P_{.i.} = Q_{...} - C_{.i.} \, , \text{ and}$$

$$(52) \qquad P_{...} = Q_{...} - C_{...} \, .$$

From Equations (34) and (42) we have immediately:

$$(53) \qquad D_{.i.}^2 = \frac{1}{nt} \sum_j \sum_h (P_{hij} - P_{.ij})^2 = 0,$$

$$(54) \qquad D_{..j}^2 = \frac{1}{Nt} \sum_i \sum_h (P_{hij} - P_{.ij})^2 = 0 \, .$$

From Statements 8a and 9a it follows then that all paired comparisons would be consistent and transitive and hence each individual would yield a simply ordered I scale. From Equations (53) and (54) it immediately follows that the phenotypic scores of individuals and stimuli would be perfectly reliable. It is not yet evident, however, that they contain any common meaning or quality in the sense of a trait as that concept has been defined by genotypic parameters. This latter information is dependent upon the quantities $T_{.i.}^2$ and $T_{..j}^2$, the two dual concepts of homogeneity. As will shortly be seen, under the conditions of class $(0, 0)_{11}$, the parameters $r_{P_{.ij}P_{..j}}$ and $r_{P_{.ij}P_{.i.}}$ are each equal to unity. Substituting these values in Equations (40) and (48), yields the result $T_{.i.}^2 = T_{..j}^2 = 0$, and the interpretation follows that in this class there is perfect homogeneity from the point of view of either individuals or stimuli.*

---

*Cf. Chapter IV, pp. 25-36.

The consequences of these two quantities, $T^2_{.i.}$ and $T^2_{..j}$, both equalling zero, are that the data, whether collected by the Method of Rank Order or by Paired Comparisons, whether in the form of I scales or S scales, will all be from a single J scale. The phenotypic behavior of all the individuals and all the stimuli can be completely represented by a single genotypic continuum on which they can be located in the sense of an ordered metric.[8]

If the data were collected by the Method of Single Stimuli, it follows from Statement 7a that a Guttman scalogram analysis would yield a perfect pattern with 100 per cent reproducibility.

It is to be anticipated, under these circumstances, that the parameters for individuals and stimuli with respect to their belongingness to their respective groups should also indicate complete belongingness. From

$$(55) \qquad r_{P_{.ij}P_{..j}} = \frac{\sum_j (P_{.ij} - P_{.i.})(P_{..j} - P_{...})}{\sqrt{\sum_j (P_{.ij} - P_{.i.})^2 \sum_j (P_{..j} - P_{...})^2}}$$

and from Equations (49), (50), (51), and (52) we have

$$(56) \qquad r_{P_{.ij}P_{..j}} =$$

$$\frac{\sum_j [(Q_{..j} - C_{.i.}) - (Q_{...} - C_{.i.})][(Q_{..j} - C_{...}) - (Q_{...} - C_{...})]}{\sqrt{\sum_j [(Q_{..j} - C_{.i.}) - (Q_{...} - C_{.i.})]^2 \sum_j [(Q_{..j} - C_{...}) - (Q_{...} - C_{...})]^2}},$$

which simplifies to

$$(57) \qquad r_{P_{.ij}P_{..j}} = \frac{\sum_j (Q_{..j} - Q_{...})(Q_{..j} - Q_{...})}{\sqrt{\sum_j (Q_{..j} - Q_{...})^2 \sum_j (Q_{..j} - Q_{...})^2}} = 1,$$

indicating the complete belongingness of each individual to the group of individuals.

Similarly

$$(58) \qquad r_{P_{.ij}P_{.i.}} = \frac{\sum_j (P_{.ij} - P_{..j})(P_{.i.} - P_{...})}{\sqrt{\sum_j (P_{.ij} - P_{..j})^2 \sum_j (P_{.i.} - P_{...})^2}},$$

49

substituting from Equations (49), (50), (51), and (52), and simplifying, yields

(59)
$$r_{P_{.ij}P_{.i.}} = 1 ,$$

indicating the complete belongingness of each stimulus to the group of stimuli.

The correlation between a pair of stimuli, e.g., j_1 and j_2, for these conditions may be obtained by making the appropriate substitutions in the following equation:

(60)
$$r_{P_{.ij_1}P_{.ij_2}} = \frac{\sum_i (P_{.ij_1} - P_{..j_1})(P_{.ij_2} - P_{..j_2})}{\sqrt{\sum_i (P_{.ij_1} - P_{..j_1})^2 \sum_i (P_{.ij_2} - P_{..j_2})^2}} .$$

substituting from Equations (49) and (50)

(61)
$$r_{P_{.ij_1}P_{.ij_2}} =$$

$$\frac{\sum_i [(Q_{..j_1} - C_{.i.}) - (Q_{..j_1} - C_{...})][(Q_{..j_2} - C_{.i.}) - (Q_{..j_2} - C_{...})]}{\sqrt{\sum_i [(Q_{..j_1} - C_{.i.}) - (Q_{..j_1} - C_{...})]^2 \sum_i [(Q_{..j_2} - C_{.i.}) - (Q_{..j_2} - C_{...})]^2}} ,$$

which reduces to

(62)
$$r_{P_{.ij_1}P_{.ij_2}} = \frac{\sum_i (C_{...} - C_{.i.})^2}{\sum_i (C_{...} - C_{.i.})^2} = 1$$

Thus all stimuli are perfectly intercorrelated.

Then, finally, the correlation between any pair of individuals, e.g., i_1, and i_2, may be obtained by making the appropriate substitutions in the following equation:

(63)
$$r_{P_{.i_1j}P_{.i_2j}} = \frac{\sum_j (P_{.i_1j} - P_{.i_1.})(P_{.i_2j} - P_{.i_2.})}{\sqrt{\sum_j (P_{.i_1j} - P_{.i_1.})^2 \sum_j (P_{.i_2j} - P_{.i_2.})^2}} .$$

50

Substituting from Equations (49) and (51) we have

(64) $\quad r_{P_{.i_1 j} P_{.i_2 j}} =$

$$\frac{\sum_j [(Q_{..j} - C_{.i_1.}) - (Q_{...} - C_{.i_1.})] \, [(Q_{..j} - C_{.i_2.}) - (Q_{...} - C_{.i_2.})]}{\sqrt{\sum_j [(Q_{..j} - C_{.i_1.}) - (Q_{...} - C_{.i_1.})]^2 \, \sum_j [(Q_{..j} - C_{.i_2.}) - (Q_{...} - C_{.i_2.})]^2}} ,$$

which reduces to

(65) $\quad r_{P_{.i_1 j} P_{.i_2 j}} = \dfrac{\sum_j (Q_{..j} - Q_{...})^2}{\sum_j (Q_{..j} - Q_{...})^2} = 1$

It might be remarked that this is the only class, $(0, 0)_{11}$, in the domain of Joint scales, for which these extreme values for the phenotypic parameters are *all* obtained in the manifest data. Thus it is apparent what the characteristics must be on the genotypic level to give rise to such data.

It is interesting to note further that

(66) $\quad r_{P_{.ij} P_{..j}} = r_{(Q_{..j} - C_{.i.}) P_{..j}} = r_{Q_{..j} P_{..j}} = 1 ,$

from which it follows that the phenotypic scale values of the stimuli, $P_{..j}$, are equal to the genotypic scale values of the stimuli, $Q_{..j}$, within a linear transformation.

Also

$\quad r_{P_{.ij} P_{.i.}} = r_{(Q_{..j} - C_{.i.}) P_{.i.}} = r_{-C_{.i.} P_{.i.}} = 1 ,$

which indicates that the phenotypic scale values of the individuals, $P_{.i.}$, are equal to the *negatives* of their genotypic scale values, $C_{.i.}$, within a linear transformation. These relationships have been shown to hold for this class, $(0, 0)_{11}$. This particular class has considerable theoretical and didactic value because of its extreme simplicity and is identical with the class called class 1 elsewhere.[8]

It should be pointed out that the development went from the genotypic level to the phenotypic level. It was demonstrated what the consequences would be to the manifest behavior for certain conditions on the genotypic level for this postulate system. Actually, however, these relationships are applied in the opposite direction. The characteristics of manifest behavior are observed; from these the characteristics of the genotypic are inferred. It has not been shown that for this given set of parameters or characteristics of the manifest data it is *necessary* that these and only these conditions must characterize the genotypic level. There is, in addition, another limitation to the interpretation of the characteristics of manifest data and this is one which is usually overlooked. The observation in a particular experiment that the quantities $D^2_{.i.}$, $D^2_{..j}$, $T^2_{.i.}$, and $T^2_{..j}$ all equal zero is not an absolute observation but a relative one. The P values on which these quantities are based are not measured, but only a crude quantitative classification of them is made or their ordered magnitude observed, depending on the method of collecting data. Consequently, the detection of a variation in the value of $P_{.ij}$ over j, for example, is dependent upon the presence of P for other stimuli sufficiently near so the the variation can be detected.

Generally speaking, the less the variability of $P_{.ij}$ for any j, the more stimuli it would be necessary to use to detect it. In different terms, for any given degree of variability of phenotypic scores, the fewer the stimuli used the less evident is the variability. This is related to the common practice of eliminating items and/or individuals in a scalogram analysis to secure a perfectly reproducible scale. In many qualitative domains such as attitudes and opinions, homogeneity is lost with more than five or six stimuli. This is not necessarily because the other stimuli are in a different domain of behavior but instead may reflect the fact that a set of stimuli constitutes an instrument for the observation of manifest behavior, and the more stimuli the more sensitive the instrument to genotypic variability.

The relations between phenotypic and genotypic parameters in the single class $(0, 0)_{11}$, have been considered in detail. More briefly, class $(0, 0)_{12}$, for which the genotypic conditions are given in Figure 1, will now be examined. This is the class in which each stimulus has one and only one genotypic scale position for all individuals. The individuals, however, have a variable genotypic scale position over time, but the mean position of an individual over a very large number of responses to a stimulus, is the same regardless of the stimulus.

This class of data represents behavior in which there is perfect homogeneity of both individuals and stimuli, but there is random variability of the genotypic scale values of individuals over time. If one had a set of arithmetic items and of individuals both perfectly homogeneous as defined here but the individuals had lapses of attention, say, in working the problems, this would correspond to class $(0, 0)_{12}$ data. The problem is to determine what the characteristics of the manifest data would be for such genotypic conditions.

From the genotypic characteristics it follows that

$$Q_{hij} = Q_{..j} \text{ and } C_{.ij} = C_{.i.} \text{ , but } C_{hij} \neq C_{.ij} \text{ .}$$

From the definitions the following values may be written for the intervening variable P :

(68)
$$P_{hij} = Q_{..j} - C_{hi.} \text{ ,}$$

(69)
$$P_{.ij} = Q_{..j} - C_{.i.} \text{ ,}$$

(70)
$$P_{..j} = Q_{..j} - C_{...} \text{ ,}$$

(71)
$$P_{.i.} = Q_{...} - C_{.i.} \text{ ,}$$

(72)
$$P_{...} = Q_{...} - C_{...} \text{ .}$$

Substituting Equations (68) and (69) into the equation for $D_{.i.}^2$, we have:

(34)
$$D_{.i.}^2 = \frac{1}{nt} \sum_j \sum_h [(Q_{..j} - C_{hi.}) - (Q_{..j} - C_{.i.})]^2$$

$$= \frac{1}{t} \sum_h (C_{.i.} - C_{hi.})^2 \text{ ,}$$

which is a variance and necessarily positive; hence $D_{.i.}^2 > 0$. Similarly, we find

(73)
$$D_{..j}^2 = \frac{1}{t} \sum_h (C_{.i.} - C_{hi.})^2 \text{ ,}$$

and hence $D_{..j}^2 > 0$.

The interpretation of the parameters $D_{.i.}^2$ and $D_{..j}^2$ was discussed

53

in the previous chapter. In summary, for both to have values greater than zero signifies that the phenotypic scale values of both individuals and stimuli are unreliable.

To determine whether $T^2_{.i.}$ and $T^2_{..j}$ are equal to zero for this class it is sufficient to observe that both $r_{P_{.ij}P_{..j}}$ and $r_{P_{.ij}P_{.i.}}$ are equal to unity. Consequently, from Equations (40) and (48) it immediately follows that $T^2_{.i.} = T^2_{..j} = 0$, the significance of which has been previously pointed out.

To complete briefly the phenotypic parameters for the class $(0, 0)_{12}$ we find for the various correlation coefficients, that

$$r_{P_{.ij}P_{..j}} = r_{P_{.ij}P_{.i.}} = r_{P_{.ij_1}P_{.ij_2}} = r_{P_{.i_1j}P_{.i_2j}} = 1 \ .$$

In summary, then, we find that the phenotypic parameters for the class $(0, 0)_{12}$ are: $D^2_{.i.} > 0$; $D^2_{..j} > 0$; $T^2_{.i.} = 0$; $T^2_{..j} = 0$; and the correlations are all equal to *one*. Here we have a situation in which all the stimuli belong to the same domain, the individuals are also homogeneous, and the inter-item and inter-individual correlations are *one*, and yet, if one collected the data by the Method of Paired Comparisons, the judgments of an individual might be intransitive and rank order I scales and S scales could not be formed. If one collected the data by the Method of Rank Order, one would, of course, create I scales or S scales as simple orders directly, but then they would appear not to constitute members of a set generated by a single common J scale. Yet, actually there is a single J scale on which each stimulus had one and only one scale position but on which the individuals had some degree of variation $(d^2_{.i.} > 0)$. This would be the class of behavior for which the Method of Triads would be well suited for the collection of data.* The handling of such data involves some intriguing problems and difficulties, which however lie outside of the scope of this monograph.

Class $(0, 0)_{13}$ is essentially equivalent to class $(0, 0)_{11}$ except that it is a class of multidimensionality among the stimuli instead of unidimensionality as in the case of class $(0, 0)_{11}$. In class $(0, 0)_{13}$ the stimuli would separate into subsets, each subset corresponding to a different J scale and the individuals on all of them. This is

---

*See in this respect Ref. 11.

the type of situation which an omnibus mental test approximates. The remaining classes of the (0, 0) grid may be studied in exactly the same manner. Results of such studies, as yet incomplete, reveal that lack of homogeneity among the stimuli on the genotypic level (i.e., if the stimuli are measuring different attributes), is sufficient to induce apparent heterogeneity of individuals on the phenotypic level. These investigations have only been begun but enough has been presented here to indicate the direction and nature of what can be done.

Chapter VII

THE UNFOLDING TECHNIQUE

The Unfolding Technique was explicitly designed to "explain" preference behavior. Existing techniques for scaling such data, as Thurstone's Law of Comparative Judgment as applied in his study of Nationality Preferences,[23] are procedures for the analysis of data of this nature for the purpose of constructing a phenotypic scale,* one which best represents the preferences of the individuals in a group in some statistical sense such as least squares (see Ref. 19). The objective of the Unfolding Technique is to go behind the expressed preferences of individuals and to construct a model from which their preferences may be *derived*. It is in this sense that the term "explain" is used. This underlying model from which the phenotypic behavior may be derived is referred to as the genotypic level of behavior.

An earlier paper[8] introduced the Unfolding Technique. In that paper J scales and I scales were defined and their relation brought out under class 1 conditions. In this chapter the discussion will be carried a little further for class 1 conditions, and then other conditions will be taken up.

Class 1 Conditions

Class 1 conditions were defined in that paper to be the conditions that each stimulus has one and only one genotypic scale position for all individuals and that each individual has one and only one genotypic scale position for all stimuli. These are the conditions that characterize class $(0, 0)_{11}$ in the $(0, 0)$ scale grid. It will now be evident that Equation (1) of the earlier paper[8] is an adaptation of Statements 6, 8a and 9a permissible under class 1 conditions. These conditions made the presentation of the Unfolding Technique simpler.

In addition to the metric relations between stimuli obtained from the Unfolding Technique for class 1 conditions, the metric relations

---

*This procedure may be regarded as one mechanism for constructing a social utility from the individuals' utilities[3].

among the regions into which the individuals are classified may also be deduced. This was indicated in the paper referred to but not demonstrated.

Consider a J scale with the stimuli in the order ABCDE. Let this be a common interval scale genotypically but only an ordered metric phenotypically. Let the unknown genotypic scale value of stimulus A be designated a . Then the scale value of the midpoint AB would be $a + \dfrac{\overline{AB}}{2}$ * , or

$$AB = \frac{2a + \overline{AB}}{2}$$

Similarly, the remaining midpoints would have scale values as follows:

$$AC = \frac{2a + \overline{AB} + \overline{BC}}{2}$$

$$AD = \frac{2a + \overline{AB} + \overline{BC} + \overline{CD}}{2}$$

$$AE = \frac{2a + \overline{AB} + \overline{BC} + \overline{CD} + \overline{DE}}{2}$$

$$BC = \frac{2a + 2\overline{AB} + \overline{BC}}{2}$$

$$BD = \frac{2a + 2\overline{AB} + \overline{BC} + \overline{CD}}{2}$$

$$BE = \frac{2a + 2\overline{AB} + \overline{BC} + \overline{CD} + \overline{DE}}{2}$$

$$CD = \frac{2a + 2\overline{AB} + 2\overline{BC} + \overline{CD}}{2}$$

$$CE = \frac{2a + 2\overline{AB} + 2\overline{BC} + \overline{CD} + \overline{DE}}{2}$$

$$DE = \frac{2a + 2\overline{AB} + 2\overline{BC} + 2\overline{CD} + \overline{DE}}{2}$$

If now, experimentally, a set of I scales were obtained which generated a common quantitative J scale, then from the metric relations

---

*The symbol $\overline{AB}$ signifies the distance between stimuli A and B.

between stimuli, something about the relative magnitudes of the regions associated with the I scales can be deduced. Suppose, for example, the following set of I scales for these five stimuli were obtained:

$$\begin{array}{c}
ABCDE \\
BACDE \\
BCADE \\
BCDAE \\
CBDAE \\
CDBAE \\
CDBEA \\
CDEBA \\
DCEBA \\
DECBA \\
EDCBA
\end{array}$$

The order of midpoints on the J scale from left to right is then: AB, AC, AD, BC, BD, AE, BE, CD, CE, DE. The first two and last two, of course, yield no information about metric relations, the remaining ones do. The following table contains the order of pairs of midpoints and the metric relations that are implied:

Order of Midpoints	Metric Relations
AD, BC	$\overline{AB} > \overline{CD}$
BD, AE	$\overline{DE} > \overline{AB}$
BE, CD	$\overline{BC} > \overline{DE}$

Putting these together, it is evident that

$$\overline{BC} > \overline{DE} > \overline{AB} > \overline{CD}$$

From this information it is now possible to say something about the metric relations of the regions bounded by the midpoints. The second region, for example, yielding the second I scale BACDE, is bounded by the midpoint AB on the left and AC on the right. Subtracting the scale value of the midpoint on the left from that of the midpoint on the right gives the magnitude of the region, in this case,

$$I_2 = AC - AB = \frac{2a + \overline{AB} + \overline{BC}}{2} - \frac{2a + \overline{AB}}{2} = \frac{\overline{BC}}{2}$$

58

Hence the width of the region associated with the second I scale is half the distance between the second and the third stimulus. Continuing with this procedure the magnitude of the various regions can be determined in terms of the magnitudes of the distances between the stimuli. The results for these hypothetical data are as follows:

Interval	Bounding Midpoints	Magnitude
I_1	unbounded on the left, AB	indeterminate
I_2	AB, AC	$\dfrac{\overline{BC}}{2}$
I_3	AC, AD	$\dfrac{\overline{CD}}{2}$
I_4	AD, BC	$\dfrac{\overline{AB} - \overline{CD}}{2}$
I_5	BC, BD	$\dfrac{\overline{CD}}{2}$
I_6	BD, AE	$\dfrac{\overline{DE} - \overline{AB}}{2}$
I_7	AE, BE	$\dfrac{\overline{AB}}{2}$
I_8	BE, CD	$\dfrac{\overline{BC} - \overline{DE}}{2}$
I_9	CD, CE	$\dfrac{\overline{DE}}{2}$
I_{10}	CE, DE	$\dfrac{\overline{CD}}{2}$
I_{11}	DE, unbounded on the right	indeterminate

From the known metric relations between the stimuli the following metric relations can be said to hold for the regions in which individuals have been classified:

59

$$I_2 > I_9 > I_7 > I_3 = I_5 = I_{10}$$

and

$$I_4 + I_6 + I_8 = \frac{\overline{BC} - \overline{CD}}{2}$$

Information of this character would be of value in testing hypotheses about the distribution function of the population on the attribute.

This concludes the treatment of class 1 data except for two points which simplify the actual handling of data.

1) To determine the metric information implied in the order of any pair of midpoints they may be written in the order in which they occur and then rewritten as two pairs, associating the first member of the first midpoint with the first member of the second midpoint to form a new pair, and then the second member of the first midpoint with the second member of the second midpoint to form the other pair. If the order of the two midpoints has metric implications one of the pairs will be in alphabetical order, the other will not. The one in alphabetical order is the larger distance.

Thus, suppose eight stimuli are on a J scale and designated alphabetically from left to right in the order ABC. . . H. If midpoint CE precedes midpoint BG, we then write CE, BG and form the two new pairs CB, EG. Observing that CB is not in alphabetical order but EG is, it follows that $\overline{EG} > \overline{BC}$.

2) The above procedure does not need to be carried out for all pairs of midpoints because there are certain necessary order relations which hold between the midpoints of a set of points on a line. Thus, if again the stimuli are designated in order on a line as ABC. . ., then the midpoints between any one with each of the others will lie in the same order as the other stimuli. For example, the midpoints of stimulus D must lie in the order AD, BD, CD, DE, DF, etc. Similarly for E, they would be in the order AE, BE, CE, DE, EF, etc. Continuing this process, it is evident that BE from amongst E's midpoints must fall between BD and DE from amongst D's midpoints. But the order relation of BE to CD would have to be determined experimentally.

Let us assume that experimentally a set of I scales has been obtained which unfolds into a common J scale and it is desired to determine the metric information in these I scales. They must first be ordered in the manner previously described and then the boundaries of each interval or region determined. These boundaries are midpoints and the midpoints must be written down in order, say, from left to right.

For example, the midpoints might be in the order

AB, AC, AD, BC, AE, AF, BD, CD, BE, CE, BF, CF, DE, DF, EF.

Obviously the first three midpoints AB, AC, AD, must be in this order, but it is not necessary that they be uninterrupted in succession: AD might have been preceded by BC. A set of midpoints whose *necessary* order is also their *successive* order will be called a "sequence". The ordered set of midpoints must next be divided into sequences, as below:

AB, AC, AD, | BC, | AE, AF, | BD, CD, | BE, CE, | BF ,CF, | DE, DF, EF.

The independent pieces of metric information are contained in the pairs of midpoints formed from the last member of one sequence and the first member of the next sequence.

These pieces of metric information are experimentally independent, but whether they are logically independent or even consistent requires examination. If they are not logically consistent, e.g., if the metric relations are intransitive, then the I scales cannot constitute a set from a common J scale.

From the data given above the experimentally independent elements of metric information are as follows:

$$AD, BC \implies \overline{AB} > \overline{CD}$$

$$BC, AE \implies \overline{CE} > \overline{AB}$$

$$AF, BD \implies \overline{AB} > \overline{DF}$$

$$CD, BE \implies \overline{DE} > \overline{BC}$$

$$CE, BF \implies \overline{EF} > \overline{BC}$$

$$CF, DE \implies \overline{CD} > \overline{EF}$$

These are readily observed to be logically independent and consistent. This procedure avoids much duplication of effort in analyzing the data. All other metric information in the data follow from the above. For example, it is observed above that $\overline{AB} > \overline{DF}$, from which it follows that $\overline{AB} > \overline{DE}$, and also that $\overline{AB} > \overline{EF}$. From this it follows that the midpoint AE must have preceded BD and that AF must have preceded BE, and this may be seen to be the case.

61

Class 2 Conditions

For convenience and simplicity of discussion the $(0, 0)_{12}$, $(0,0)_{13}$, and $(0, 0)_{14}$ classes of the $(0, 0)$ grid will be lumped together and referred to as class 2 data. The common characteristics of such data are that each stimulus would have one and only one scale position (Q value) for all individuals, but each individual would have more than one scale position (C value) over the set of stimuli. This is the type of situation approximated by an omnibus mental test containing among others, an arithmetic item and a verbal analogies item. Each of the items might tend to have one and only one Q value over all the individuals, but an individual, in going from one item to another, would take scale values on different *attributes* and would have different C values. It is apparent from the genotypic parameters for this class that it is characterized by the fact that

$$\sigma_{\substack{Q_{hij} \\ h,i}} = 0 \; ; \; \sigma_{\substack{C_{hij} \\ h,j}} > 0$$

In conventional terminology, class 2 is characterized by the fact that each stimulus is homogeneous over the individuals but that the individuals are unreliable and/or heterogeneous over the stimuli.

An attempt was made to illustrate this class of data with an experiment. This was accomplished to an approximate degree in the following experiment called the temperature-moisture experiment. In the Spring of 1950, the 40 members of a class in advanced statistics were given eight stimulus words by the Method of Paired Comparisons. These words were wet, damp, humid, dry, hot, warm, cool, cold. Each member of the class was instructed to select some activity he liked to engage in, such as swimming, skiing, sitting before a fire and reading, fishing, picnicking, hiking, etc. He was then asked to choose from each pair of words that which he would prefer as descriptive of the kind of day in which he would engage in that activity.

It was expected that four of these words would represent points on a temperature continuum (hot, warm, cool, cold) and the other four would represent points on a moisture continuum (wet, damp, humid, dry). Furthermore it was expected that an individual, having a given activity in mind, would have an ideal (see Statement 5, Chapter III) on each of these continua. If such conditions were met the data would be class 2 data. The results did not bear this out, primarily because the stimulus word "humid" had a variety of scale positions over the individuals.

The paired comparisons were transitive for 30 of the individuals and intransitive for 10. In the idealized situation where each individual had a scale position on each of the two attributes and each of the stimuli had a scale position on only one of the attributes, the paired comparisons of each individual would be transitive and would yield a rank order I scale. The I scale of an individual would be a merger of two I scales, one from each continuum. As an illustration, let the stimuli be labelled as in Figure 2.

A	B	C	D
hot	warm	cool	cold

E	F	G	H
dry	humid	damp	wet

Figure 2.

One individual, who chose "fishing" as his activity, yielded the transitive I scale: FGHBCEDA which can be seen to be a merger of the two constituent I scales

FGHE

BCDA

It is obvious that in class 2 data the I scales would not constitute a set from a common J scale, as in this case, there were I scales ending in A, D, E, or H.*

It would be extremely difficult, in general, to explore such I scales to try to find the constituent I scales and separate them. In this case it was possible because of the a priori basis for constructing the two J scales. The two sets of constituents I scales were obtained and unfolded.

In the case of the temperature continuum a common qualitative J scale for the four stimuli was obtained for 38 of the 40 individuals. In the case of the moisture continuum no common qualitative J scale was obtained. For some individuals humid was between wet and damp and for some it was between damp and dry.

The distribution of the individuals' ideals on the temperature continuum was unimodal and symmetrical, but on the moisture experiment

---

*The unfolding of such I scales would require the further development of multidimensional unfolding along the lines taken by J. F. Bennett.[4]

it was highly skewed, 34 of the 40 individuals being nearer to "dry" than any of the other three moisture stimuli. A consequence of this will be brought out in the next chapter in relation to an analysis of the same data by the Law of Comparative Judgment.

The experiment described above typifies class 2 data except for the stimulus "humid" for which $\sigma_{h,j}Q_{hij}$ was clearly greater than zero.

In principle, when the genotypic parameters meet the conditions for class 2, the I scales obtained cannot be unfolded. Instead under these conditions it is S scales that should be obtained, corresponding to I scales, but with the roles of stimuli and individuals reversed. The S scales would separate into two or more sets, each generating its own J scale. Unfortunately no way has yet been devised to get stimuli to make paired comparisons between individuals without making assumptions about a common unit of measurement.

Class 3 Conditions

Again we return to the (0, 0) scale grid and form a class of genotypic parameters symmetric to those of class 2. This class will be designated class 3 and will comprise classes $(0, 0)_{21}$, $(0, 0)_{31}$, and $(0, 0)_{41}$. The common characteristics of the genotypic parameters here are that they meet the conditions

$$\sigma_{h,i}Q_{hij} > 0 \; ; \; \sigma_{h,j}C_{hij} = 0$$

These parameters represent the condition that each individual had one and only one scale position over the stimuli, but each of the stimuli had a number of scale positions over the individuals. It is difficult to find an example of this, but it could be illustrated by a hypothetical example as follows: Imagine a number of presidential candidates as stimuli with scale positions on each of several attributes such as liberalism and internationalism. Imagine a number of voters such that some of the voters choose their ideal candidate only on the basis of internationalism. The duality of this class with class 2 is obvious and everything said about class 2 now holds for class 3 with the role of individuals and stimuli reversed, e.g., there would be several sets of I scales, each set unfolding into a J scale, but the S scales would be mergers of constituent S scales.

64

Class 5 Conditions

The remainder of the classes in the (0, 0) grid will be taken together as class 5. (The omission of class 4 is deliberate. The numbering of classes is based on a further generalization of the scale grid to include Stimulus (psychophysical) scales, Population scales, and Field scales, as well as Joint scales. This extension will be developed in a separate paper.)

From the (0, 0) grid it is evident that the common characteristics of class 5 data are that

$$\sigma_{h,i}Q_{hij} > 0 \;\; ; \;\; \sigma_{h,j}C_{hij} > 0 .$$

Whereas class 1 is a combination of the best features (from the point of simple measurement) of classes 2 and 3, class 5 is a combination of their worst features. It is unfortunately only too true that the majority of behavior which psychologists regard as interesting and significant would lie in class 5. The data of class 5 vary from data which may yield a unidimensional solution, with the variance of the individuals being within stimuli only (and the dual), to requiring a multidimensional solution, with the variance of individuals being both within and between stimuli (and the dual). The essential character of the problem here is whether to tolerate a unidimensional solution with error variance or a multidimensional solution.

Curiously enough, this problem is usually resolved on a priori grounds with the assistance of statistical criteria like reliability indices. It is usually assumed that, if one has significant reliability for a measuring instrument, "something" is being measured which is essentially unidimensional with a lot of error. The presence of reliability is not a *sufficient* condition for this interpretation.

It is precisely for such a problem as this that the parameters presented in Chapters IV and V were developed. The basic problem here was to break down an individual's genotypic variance into within-stimuli and between-stimuli components (bearing on reliability and homogeneity, respectively) and to study the relation of these genotypic components to the characteristics of the manifest data (Chapter VI). This work is still incomplete, but it is apparent that there are methods of collecting data which contain information of assistance in differentiating between unidimensional and multidimensional solutions. These methods include the Method of Paired Comparisons and the Method of

Triads. Consider, for example, the information in the separate judgments of the Method of Paired Comparisons. Assume for illustrative purposes a J scale for the stimuli ABCD as in Figure 3 and that some individual

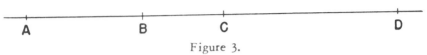

Figure 3.

has expressed his preferences with the following paired comparison judgments:

$$C > B, C > A, C > D, B > A, B > D, A > D$$

These paired comparative judgments are transitive and correspond to a rank order I scale CBAD. Next consider the individual judgments. The judgment that C was preferred to B contains the information that at the time of making that judgment, stimulus C was nearer the individual's ideal than stimulus B. Thus, the individual's ideal was on the right side of the midpoint between stimulus C and B. This has been indicated in Figure 4 with an arrow pointing in the direction of the individual's ideal.

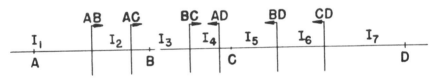

Figure 4.

In a similar manner, each paired comparison judgment merely indicates which side of a line dichotomizing the attribute the judge's ideal was when making that judgment. Each of the six judgments is indicated in the Figure by an appropriate arrow. It is evident that all these arrows point to a common interval and the inference may be made that this is the interval in which may be located the judge's ideal.

The question might be asked, could the individual have been anywhere else on the continuum and have made these same judgments? Yes, he might have been roaming over the continuum, from one end to the other and been ''caught'' on each judgment so that they all pointed at the same interval.

The probability that an individual could range or roam all over the continuum and give a set of transitive judgments is inversely related to the number of stimuli and is less probable for some methods of collecting

data than for other methods for a given number of stimuli.
In the method of single stimuli, task A, monotone stimuli, for example, with n = 10, there would be only 10 judgments made by an individual, and only if the order of the stimuli on the J scale were known could one tell whether 10 judgments were all pointing to a common interval. In the Method of Paired Comparisons 10 stimuli would require 45 judgments and transitivity of the judgments would (1) be observable without knowledge of a J scale and (2) be less probable by chance. In the Method of Triads these same 10 stimuli would have required 120 judgments and would again have an internal criterion and be still less probable by chance.

There is still a further distinction to be made between the Method of Paired Comparisons and the Method of Triads. In the Method of Paired Comparisons each judgment is made *once*, in the Method of Triads, each paired comparison judgment is made n–2 times. Thus the Method of Paired Comparisons permits transitivity and intransitivity to be distinguished, assuming consistency of the judgments. (This is from the point of view of accepting the data and making no assumptions about "errors" in order to fit the data into an a priori preferred model. One could, of course, assume transitivity, and then intransitivity would be classified as inconsistency or "error". In this case a theory is accepted and the data are weeded out to fit.) Making each paired comparison judgment n–2 times in the Method of Triads provides a basis for evaluating consistency and distinguishing intransitivity from inconsistency.

This discussion was begun with respect to the problem of unidimensional versus multidimensional unfolding with more or less error. It has been stated that the Method of Paired Comparisons and Method of Triads contain information of assistance in differentiating between the two solutions. We are now in a position to discuss this directly. Consider again the individual described earlier who made the six paired comparison judgments:

$$C > B, C > A, C > D, B > A, B > D, A > D$$

and was located in I_4. What would happen if he had changed *one* of these judgments? One of two events is observed:

1) The paired comparisons remain transitive and the individual has an I scale in an adjacent interval. (Changing $C > B$ to $B > C$ makes the I scale BCAD corresponding to I_3; changing $A > D$ to $D > A$ makes the I scale CBDA corresponding to I_5.)

2) The paired comparisons become intransitive.

From this it is apparent that if an individual were "wiggling" over two adjacent intervals on a J scale, the Method of Paired Comparisons would "catch" him in one of them and pin him down with a transitive I scale. If the paired comparisons are intransitive, this can be the consequence of wiggling over *at least* three adjacent intervals. Thus, if an individual had made the judgments

$$C > B, \; C > D, \; B > A, \; B > D, \; A > C, \; A > D,$$

his I scale would be intransitive and would be represented by a partial order of the form

$$
\begin{array}{ccc}
A & B & C \\
\diagdown & | & \diagup \\
 & D & \\
\end{array}
$$

The information in each of the six judgments is indicated by arrows in Figure 5 and their intransitivity is evident.

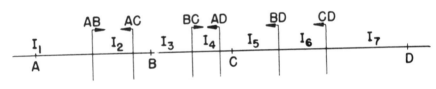

Figure 5

It would be inferred from these data that the individual's ideals varied from I_2 to I_4 on this J scale. Interpretations of this sort will be illustrated by the experiment which follows. The extent to which an interpretation of this character for intransitive or partially ordered I scales is permissible would be a function of the range the individual wiggles over in relation to the total range.

The Method of Triads is an even more searching method in this regard because it permits the estimation of an actual distribution function for an individual over the intervals. In this method each paired comparison judgment is made n–2 times, and hence, for each midpoint, the proportion of times the individual's ideal was on each side of each midpoint can be calculated. This information in combination with information on metric relations would permit an approximation to a distribution function.

68

Presumably a unimodal symmetric distribution over the scale would support an interpretation of "wiggling on a unidimensional continuum."

There are other considerations which indicate that the problem is even more complicated. One might argue that the stimuli may wiggle as well as or instead of the individual. The individual may stand with a constant ideal but the Q values of the stimuli may vary for him. As yet only one basis has been found which might be used to determine whether it is stimuli or individuals that are wiggling. If the Q values of the stimuli are varying, then pairs of stimuli on one side of an individual's ideal will tend to be reversed in order and yield inconsistent paired comparisons in the Method of Triads.

If the individual is wiggling, then this is like the hinge on the folded J scale moving back and forth, and stimuli which are bilaterally approximately equally distant will be inconsistently judged. Wiggling of the individual will have no effect on the inconsistency of judgments on pairs of stimuli which are unilaterally located on the J scale except for those in the neighborhood of the hinge. This is illustrated by Figures 6 and 7.

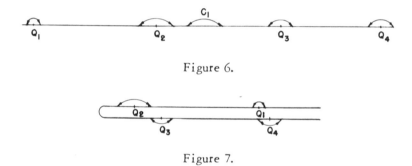

Figure 6.

Figure 7.

Comparisons between Q_1 and Q_2 or between Q_3 or Q_4 will be unchanged by the wiggling of C_1, but comparisons between Q_2 and Q_3 or between Q_1 and Q_4 will be considerably affected.

Class 5 data has been discussed mostly in the abstract and will next be illustrated with an experiment.

Cutler's Experiment on Income Expectations

This is an experiment conducted at the master's degree level by Richard L. Cutler. Its primary purpose was to illustrate experimentally a relation derived from theory between a J scale obtained by unfolding and a Group scale obtained by the Law of Comparative Judgment. This relation will be studied in detail in the next chapter. The analysis of his data by the Unfolding Technique will be considered here as an illustration of Class 5 data.

The subjects for this experiment, conducted in January, 1950, were 106 graduating seniors at the University of Michigan, majoring or minoring in psychology; there were 72 males and 34 females. Each individual was given a 30-page questionnaire as follows:

p. 1. "Instructions: This is an experiment to test certain theoretical aspects of psychological scaling techniques. It is entirely voluntary and you need not answer the questionnaire if you so choose. However, you, as an individual, will not be identified. Complete anonymity is preserved. We are interested *only* in certain internal relations in the data. This will become obvious to you because it will appear that we are getting the same information in several different ways.

"You are free, of course, to mark these items entirely at random. It is our hope, however, that you will take a serious attitude toward the experiment and make an effort to respond to each item on the basis of considered judgment.

"The questions pertain to your future income expectations. On each of the following pages you will find two numbers, each of which represents yearly income in dollars. You are to *encircle* the one which best represents what you think you will be worth to a prospective employer in your field the first year after you receive your bachelor's degree. Answer every item. Work quickly."

p. 2 to 29. On each of pages 2 - 29 was a pair of stimuli (listed below) with the following instructions:

"Circle the one in each pair which best represents what you think you will be worth."

p. 30 "What specific numerical value did you have in mind in making your judgments?"

$ _____

Age _____   Sex _____   Major Field _____

There were eight stimuli, which will be labelled as follows:

A -	$ 800	E -	$3300
B -	1300	F -	3900
C -	2000	G -	4400
D -	2600	H -	4800

Clearly these stimuli form a simply ordered scale. What will make the data Class 5 is the fact that different individuals have different metric

70

relations among these stimuli so $_{h,i}^{\sigma}Q_{hij} > 0$ and the same individuals wiggled on the continuum so $_{h,j}^{\sigma}C_{hij} > 0$.

One of the individuals was discarded for failing to respond to one of the paired comparison judgments. Of the 105 remaining subjects, the paired comparison judgments of 77 were transitive and 28 intransitive. The analysis of the transitive I scales will be made first and then the partially ordered I scales will be examined.

Five of the transitive I scales were: 1, GEFHDCBA; 1, EGFHDCBA; 2, HFGEDCBA; and 1, DECABFGH. While these five are perhaps the result of an error in making one of the paired comparison judgments there is no objective way in the Method of Paired Comparisons of testing the consistency of an individual's judgments. So rather than designate a particular judgment as an error on the part of each of these individuals in order to revise their I scales to suit an a priori notion of what they should have done, these five cases will be dropped from further consideration.

The transitive I scales of the remaining 72 individuals appear to come from a common qualitative J scale with the simple order ABCDEF-GH. These scales are listed in Table I. On the left are the intervals in order from 1 to 29 associated with corresponding I scales. The numbers in parentheses indicate the frequency of a particular I scale. Blank rows indicate the absence of an I scale in the experimental data. Of the 72 individuals, the I scales of 61 of them can be unfolded into a single quantitative J scale and these are the I scales down the center of the table. The I scales on the two sides are from the same qualitative J scale but with different metric relations. The slanting lines tying these I scales into the central list indicate the possible alternative *sets* of I scales that could be constructed corresponding to different quantitative J scales. In summary, there is one quantitative J scale which can be constructed to accommodate 61 of the 77 individuals; any other quantitative J scale would accommodate fewer than these.

It will next be of interest to determine the metric relations of the dominant quantitative J scale. To accomplish this the midpoints are listed in the order in which they occur on the J scale and this order is divided into sequences. This has been done in Table II.

71

Table I.

Partial Order of Transitive I Scales*

```
 1                    A B C D E F G H( 1 )
 2                    B A C D E F G H( 1 )
 3                       ,
 4
 5                    C B D A E F G H( 1 )
 6                    C B D E A F G H( 2 )
 7                                        \
 8                  ,C D B E F A G H( 1 )  \
 9                 /                        C B D E F G H A( 1 )
10              /      D C E B F A G H( 3 )/
11  C D E F B G A H( 1 )
12              \      D C E B F G H A( 1 )
13               \
14
15
16  F E D C B A G H( 1 )  \
17     E D F G C B A H\ ( 1 ) D E F C G H B A( 1 )\
18                 |      E D F C G H B A( 4 )      \
19     E D F C G B H A \( 1 ) E F D C G H B A( 6 )   D E F G H C B A( 1 )
20                      \     E F D G C H B A( 1 )
21                       \    E F D G H C B A( 1 )    F E D G C H B A( 2 )
22                        \   E F G D H C B A( 5 )    |
23                         \  E F G H D C B A( 8 )    F G E D C H B A( 1 )
24                           'F E G H D C B A( 5 )   /
25                            F G E H D C B A( 2 )
26                            F G H E D C B A( 3 )    G F E H D C B A( 2 )
27                            G F H E D C B A( 1 )
28
29                            H G F E D G B A( 14 )
```

*Numbers in parentheses are frequencies.

72

Table II

AB,AC,	AD / BC	AE	AF / BD	BE / CD	AG / AH	BF,BG,BH / CE,CF	DE,DF	CG,CH	DG,DH	EF,EG,EH	FG,FH,GH

It is apparent from Table II that some of the sequences are partially ordered; this is a consequence of the fact that the experimental data did not contain a complete set of I scales from this quantitative J scale. The experimentally independent pieces of metric information contained in the above order of I scales is given in Table III.

Table III

Cutler's Metric Relations

Order of Midpoints	Metric Relations
BC,AE	$\overline{CE} > \overline{AB}$
AE,BD	$\overline{AB} > \overline{DE}$
AF,BE	$\overline{AB} > \overline{EF}$
AF,CD	$\overline{AC} > \overline{DF}$
BE,AG	$\overline{EG} > \overline{AB}$
CD,AG	$\overline{DG} > \overline{AC}$
AH,BF	$\overline{AB} > \overline{FH}$
AH,CE	$\overline{AC} > \overline{EH}$
BH,DE	$\overline{BD} > \overline{EH}$
CF,DE	$\overline{CD} > \overline{EF}$
DF,CG	$\overline{FG} > \overline{CD}$
CH,DG	$\overline{CD} > \overline{GH}$
DH,EF	$\overline{DE} > \overline{FH}$
EH,FG	$\overline{EF} > \overline{GH}$

A study of these metric relations indicates that they are logically consistent, and a partial order of the metric relations may be constructed, as in Figure 8. This Figure does not contain *all* the metric relations but it does contain the experimentally and logically independent ones with a few derived relations also. An example of the latter type is the line which indicates that $\overline{DF}$, a double interval, is greater than $\overline{\overline{EH}}$, a triple interval. This follows from the fact that $\overline{DE} > \overline{\overline{FH}}$. Adding $\overline{EF}$ to both sides we have $\overline{DF} > \overline{\overline{EH}}$.

73

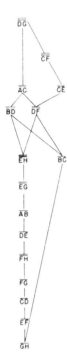

Figure 8.

As a matter of psychological interest and to facilitate interpretation the symbols in Figure 8 have been replaced by their monetary equivalents and presented in Figure 9. It is apparent that no simple arithmetic or logarithmic relation on the change in dollars corresponds to the change in psychological magnitude. It appears that the first digit has a psychological value all its own. For example, it may be seen that the $500 increment from 3900 to 4400 is greater psychologically than the $600 increment from 3300 to 3900.

It will next be of interest to see if the intransitive I scales can be accommodated on this same quantitative J scale by assuming that the individual's ideal varies over a segment of the J scale.

One individual yields the partially ordered I scale:

$$
\begin{array}{c}
D \\
\text{EF G CBA} \\
H
\end{array}
$$

An examination of this individual's responses to the questionnaire items showed that they could be accounted for on the basis of his moving on the continuum from interval 21 to interval 23 while making his judgments. This is an uncertainty of three intervals.

Another subject gave the intransitive I scale

$$
\begin{array}{c}
D \; B \; A \\
C \qquad H \\
E \; F \; G
\end{array}
$$

To account for his responses it was necessary to assume that he moved from intervals 7 to 15, a distance of 9 intervals.

Of the 28 individuals with intransitive paired comparisons, 27 can be accommodated by assuming variability of their ideals over intervals of the dominant J scale, as indicated in Table IV. The variability of the 28th individual could not be estimated because it covered some portion of the range of intervals from 13 to 17, and the data on which the dominant J scale is based do not provide information on the order of midpoints in this range. It appears then that at least 88 of the original 106 individuals can be accommodated on the same quantitative J scale.

74

Table IV

No. of intervals	No. of individuals
3	5
4	2
5	4
6	1
7	5
8	1
9	3
10	2
11	1
14	1
17	1
20	1
Total	27

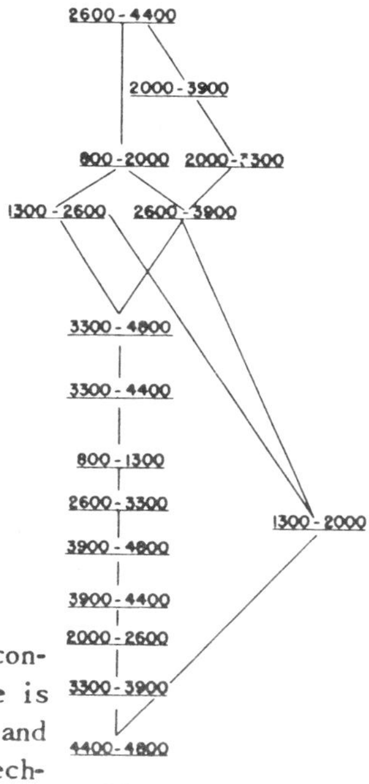

Figure 9.

The experiments discussed in this chapter were conducted primarily for a different purpose—this purpose is the subject of the next chapter. These experiments and some others will be analyzed there by a different technique; the Law of Comparative Judgment which will provide an entirely different point of view. The relation between an analysis of preference data by the Law of Comparative Judgment and by unfolding will be derived and demonstrated experimentally.

Chapter VIII.

SOME IMPLICATIONS FOR THE LAW
OF COMPARATIVE JUDGMENT

In this chapter certain immediate consequences and implications of the Statements will be presented. One consequence was the new Unfolding Technique presented in an earlier paper[8] and developed further in Chapter VII. There are interesting relations and differences between that scaling technique and the well-known one of Thurstone's Law of Comparative Judgment. The Unfolding Technique may be used in the scaling of stimuli which have macroscopic differences and are discriminable. The Law of Comparative Judgment is dependent upon discriminal error for its unit of measurement. In the Unfolding Technique there is no unit of measurement, and hence the solution is not in numerical scale values. Another very important characteristic of the Unfolding Technique that should be explicitly pointed out is that it by no means guarantees a solution or a scale. In fact, quite the contrary. Limited but consistent experience has shown that a single Joint scale (see Chapter VII) satisfying *all* the responses (task A) of a group of individuals to a group of stimuli rarely, if ever, occurs. While this will be regarded as a defect by many measurement people, the writer's feeling in this matter is expressed by the conviction that scales should be *sought*, not *made*. Unidimensional scales are desirable because they provide measuring instruments, but more important than this is that the mere fact of the existence of a scale, or the degree to which a scale exists, has social-psychological significance.[7] If, however, an interval scale is desired for technological reasons to serve as a common measuring instrument for some qualitative attribute such as an attitude, there may be nothing better than a scale developed by the Law of Comparative Judgment or one of its derivatives.[22]

One other characteristic of the Unfolding Technique is that only one experimental operation is necessary for the scaling of both individuals and stimuli on a Joint scale. It is possible to add the necessary postulates to this system so that a numerical solution analogous to the Law of Comparative Judgment can be found for a Joint scale computed from data collected by task A. These equations have been developed, but their practical utility has not been investigated.

From Statement 9 certain relations between the Unfolding Technique and the Law of Comparative Judgment can be developed. These relations lead to interesting reinterpretations of a scale developed by the Law of Comparative Judgment and to some predictions which are susceptible of experimental verification. In particular, it will be shown that there are two distinct Laws of Comparative Judgment which have known mathematical relations between them, and these relations will be tested experimentally.

The distinction between the two Laws of Comparative Judgment is based upon the two different tasks which individuals may be asked to perform when the data are collected by the Method of Paired Comparisons. These two tasks are task A and task B (Statement 2), judgments of preference and judgments with respect to an attribute, respectively. These two kinds of data require two Laws of Comparative Judgment because of the different kinds of information contained in the responses (Statements 9a and 9b).

The first Law of Comparative Judgment will now be derived and will pertain to the scaling of data collected by the Method of Paired Comparisons, task A. Such data are exemplified by Thurstone's study of nationality preferences[23] and any other set of paired comparisons involving the preferences of individuals.

From Statement 9a it immediately follows that when an individual is given two stimuli, j and k, to choose between, the individual will make the judgment: "j preferred to k" if and only if $|P_{hij}| \leq |P_{hik}|$. The proportion of times that the judgment "j preferred to k" is made is the proportion of times that

(74) $$|P_{hik}| - |P_{hij}| \geq 0.$$

The series of judgments may be over h for a given i (Thurstone's Case I) or over i for a given h (Thurstone's Case II).

Case I of the First Law: If the data are collected over h for a given i, a distribution may be constructed of values of equation (74) over h. The mean of this distribution is

(75) $$|P|_{\cdot ik} - |P|_{\cdot ij},$$

where

(76) $$|P|_{\cdot ij} = \frac{1}{t} \sum_{h} |P|_{hij},$$

77

and the variance will be designated

(77)
$$\sigma^2 |P|_{.ik} - |P|_{.ij}.$$

The parallel with the Law of Comparative Judgment is evident from the equation

(78)
$$|P|_{.ij} - |P|_{.ik} = X_{.i,jk}\, \sigma |P|_{.ik} - |P|_{.ij},$$

where $X_{.i,jk}$ is the sigma score for a difference of zero (equation 75) between stimuli j and k for a given i over h.

Case II of the First Law: If the data are collected over i for a given h, the new equation analogous to (78), derived in a similar manner, is

(79)
$$|P|_{h\cdot j} - |P|_{h\cdot k} = X_{h\cdot,jk}\, \sigma |P|_{h\cdot j} - |P|_{h\cdot k},$$

where the dot indicates, as before, a subscript removed by averaging.

Rather than proceed with an interpretation at this point, it is better to derive the Second Law of Comparative Judgment, and then the interpretations will be clearer for the distinction.

The Second Law of Comparative Judgment pertains to the scaling of data collected by the Method of Paired Comparisons, task B. In general terms the data consist of judgments as to which of every pair of stimuli has more of some attribute.

The information contained in such data is defined by Statement 9b. It immediately follows that when an individual is given two stimuli, j and k, to evaluate with respect to some attribute, the individual will make the judgment "stimulus j has more of *(some attribute)* than stimulus k" if and only if

$$P_{hij} \geq P_{hik}.$$

The proportion of times this judgment is made is then simply the proportion of times that

(80)
$$P_{hij} - P_{hik} \geq 0.$$

This series of judgments may be over h for a given i (Case I) or over i for a given h (Case II).

Case I of the Second Law of Comparative Judgment: If the data are collected over h for a given i, a distribution may be constructed of values of Equation (80) over h. The mean of this distribution is

$$(81) \qquad P_{\cdot ij} - P_{\cdot ik},$$

and the variance is designated

$$(82) \qquad \sigma^2{}_{P_{\cdot ij} - P_{\cdot ik}}$$

Again an equation precisely analogous to the Law of Comparative Judgment may be written:

$$(83) \qquad P_{\cdot ij} - P_{\cdot ik} = X_{\cdot i, jk}\, \sigma_{P_{\cdot ij} - P_{\cdot ik}},$$

where $X_{\cdot i, jk}$ is the sigma score for a difference of zero (Equation (81)) between stimuli j and k for a given i over h.

Case II of the Second Law of Comparative Judgment: If the data are collected over i for a given h the new equation analogous to (83) derived in an identical manner, is

$$(84) \qquad P_{h \cdot j} - P_{h \cdot k} = X_{h \cdot, jk}\, \sigma_{P_{h \cdot j} - P_{h \cdot k}},$$

and it is now evident that there are fundamentally two Laws of Comparative Judgment for each of which there are two forms corresponding to Case I and Case II.

If, then, one were able to estimate the Q and C values of stimuli and individuals, even crudely and approximately, one could compute, on the basis of the statements, for the appropriate kind of data, theoretical scale values for the stimuli. If, then, at the same time, the paired comparison judgments of the individuals were obtained, one could compute scale values by means of the appropriate Law of Comparative Judgment above, with the additional assumptions and approximations involved in applying the Law of Comparative Judgment, and these two solutions should have a reasonable degree of relation. In some of the experiments described in this chapter this has been done, and the additional experiments are for the purpose of illustrating the particular interpretation to be given to a solution by Equation (79), discussed in the next section.

79

The Group Scale

It is apparent from Equation (79) that the phenotypic scale values of stimuli, $|P|_{h \cdot j}$, $|P|_{h \cdot k}$, etc., represent the arithmetic mean of the scale values of each stimulus over the individuals' I scales. This "mean" scale, then, is an average of all the I scales and is a popularity or preference scale for the group of individuals taken as a whole.[*] For this reason, such a scale will be called a Group scale. The Group scale then is one with the stimuli scaled from left to right in oraer of decreasing group preference, just as in an I scale of an individual, and in fact, it is nothing more than an average of the I scales.

With this definition and, if at the same time the I scales of a group of individuals were all generated from a common J scale, then the Group scale would be a J scale folded at the median of the individuals' C values or ideals on the J scale.

The Group scale may be interpreted as a scale of social choice or social utility in that it is passing from a set of individual utilities to a group or social utility based on the value judgment that social utility is a sum or average of the individual utilities.[**]

Defining a Group scale as the mean of all the I scales, the scale secured by the application of Equation (79) by means of case V of the Law of Comparative Judgment, may be regarded as an approximation to this Group scale. The conventional solution to Equation (79) would be an approximation because of the assumptions of Case V, i.e. that the standard deviation of the differences, $|P_{hij}| - |P_{hik}|$, over all pairs j,k is constant, that the differences were normally distributed, and that application of the Law of Comparative Judgment weights preferences monotonically proportional to their "popularity."

The experimental test of such a predicted relation is then easily designed. The paradigm involves two independent analyses of the same data, which should bear a predicted relation to each other:

1) The data should consist of the paired comparison judgments by each of a number of different individuals under task A.

2) The data would be analyzed independently by the Unfolding Technique and by the Law of Comparative Judgment.

3) If the I scales of the individuals unfold into a common J scale the Group scale obtained by the Law of Comparative Judgment should tend to approximate the J scale folded at the median individual.

---

[*]This is a mechanism for defining a social utility giving every individual an equal voice but weighting the "strength" of each preference.

[**]In this context see Ref. 3, p. 4.

The following experiments are attempts to meet these conditions to see if the predicted relation holds.

The Beauty Experiment

This experiment was conducted in the Fall of 1950 with 105 subjects, both undergraduate and graduate, obtained from several psychology courses at the University of Michigan. The stimuli used were eight adjectives representing degrees of beauty: gorgeous, alluring, beautiful, lovely, attractive, good-looking, pretty, and comely. It was necessary for the purposes of this experiment that the individual judges have ideals on the attribute continuum represented by these adjectives. This could have been done in a number of ways and was done artificially in order to construct an approximately rectangular distribution of the individuals' ideals. In order to accomplish this, each individual was assigned one of the stimulus words as a standard (ideal), and he judged which member of every pair of other stimulus words had more nearly the same meaning as his criterion word.

To analyze the data by the Unfolding Technique each individual's judgments would have to be converted into I scales (simply or partially ordered) and unfolded. This analysis revealed the absence of any common qualitative J scale for all individuals. From additional data collected in the same experiment by the Method of Similarities[11] it was apparent that each of a number of individuals had a single unidimensional structure underlying these adjectives but that this structure was not a common one. For example for some individuals "pretty" was more than "attractive," for others the reverse, and similar disagreements *between* individuals occurred between pairs of words formed from the group: comely, good-looking, attractive, and pretty.

This disagreement on the order of words in the Unfolded J scale existed only between words whose differences in meaning were relatively slight. In general there were three clearly distinguished classes of words (1) gorgeous, alluring, and beautiful were always the highest three but in somewhat varying order for different individuals; (2) lovely constituted the middle class all by itself; (3) attractive, good-looking, pretty, and comely constituted the third class, which in varying order were always the last four.

The paired comparison judgments of the individuals were then analyzed by Case V of the Law of Comparative Judgment and the result on a scale running from zero to ten is indicated in Figure 10.

It is evident that this group scale could represent a J scale folded in the neighborhood of "lovely." The location of the "median" individual,

81

Figure 10.

at the folding point, would be in I_{13}, bounded by the midpoint between "attractive" and "lovely" on one side and the midpoint between "attractive" and "beautiful" on the other side. This suggests that this Group scale could be unfolded to yield a J scale. The unfolded J scale is shown in Figure 11 with the spacing between adjacent stimuli indicated.

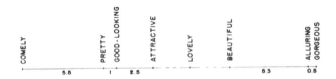

Figure 11.

The break in the scale in the neighborhood of "lovely" is a consequence of the lack of information about the precise relation between the stimulus "lovely" and the hinge.* This experiment has been analyzed in sufficient detail to sustain in a qualitative manner the predicted relation that a Group scale is a folded J scale under the appropriate conditions.

---

*Having the paired comparison judgments of individuals as to which of each pair of statements of opinion each person would prefer to indorse, there is the implication in the above that a Group scale could be unfolded into a J scale and hence both stimuli and individuals located on a common continuum in one experimental operation. This implication is correct, particularly as a technique has been developed which permits the location of the hinge and hence the determination of the magnitude of the two intervals left uncertain in the above analysis. However, further study has revealed that the metric relations of the unfolded Group scale (obtained by the Law of Comparative Judgment) are sensitive to the frequency distribution of ideals on the J scale, which is not a desirable feature for building an attitude continuum.

Temperature-Moisture Experiment

The conclusion that a Group scale is a folded J scale may be drawn only when all the I scales of which the Group scale is a mean generate a common J scale. If the I scales come not from a single J scale, but as may be the case under class 2 conditions, come from two or more J scales, then each individual's I scale is a merger of his constituent I scales each from a distinct attribute continuum. Such composite I scales were discussed in detail in the previous chapter in the section on class 2 conditions and were illustrated by the temperature-moisture experiment.

The analysis of these same data will now be continued from an entirely different point of view and the relation between a Group scale and multiple J scales indicated. Recalling again that a Group scale is defined as the mean of all the I scales, then, if such I scales are mergers of constituent I scales, the Group scale should obviously be the merger of constituent Group scales.

As each individual made each of the paired comparison judgments between the eight stimuli—wet, damp, humid, dry, hot, warm, cool, and cold—from the point of view of some predefined activity, a Law of Comparative Judgment, Case V, solution to these data was computed.

The paired comparison solution is indicated in Figure 12.

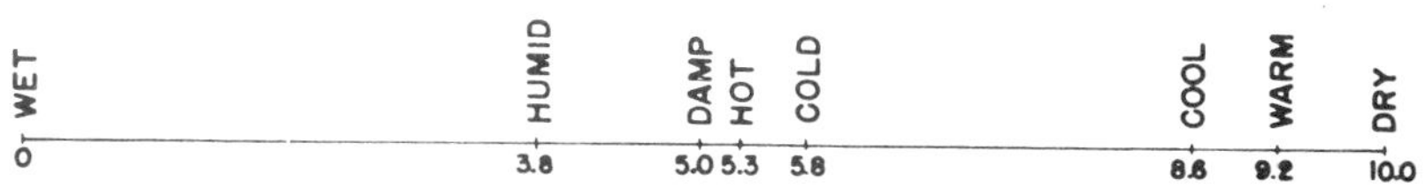

Figure 12.

It is evident here that the two constituent Group scales here consist of the stimuli in the order

a) dry, damp, humid, wet
b) warm, cool, cold, hot.

It will be recalled that the distribution of the individuals on the unfolded J scales was unimodal and symmetrical on the temperature continuum and very highly skewed on the moisture continuum, in the latter instance 34 out of the 40 cases were nearer to "dry" than to any of the other three stimuli. Inasmuch as the Group scale is a mean of the I scales, then, provided the I scales are from a common J scale, the Group scale is the I scale of the "median" individual on the J scale.

Thus, the moisture Group scale has the stimuli in the same order as the J scale for moisture, and the temperature Group scale is folded in the neighborhood of the stimulus "warm." These two constituent Group scales have then been merged into a Group scale which is approximated by the Law of Comparative Judgment.

The last two experiments have been illustrative of the derived relation between a Group scale computed by the Law of Comparative Judgment and a J space. In the two remaining experiments an attempt will be made to make a quantitative study of this relation and in addition test some of the basic postulates described in Chapter III.

Cutler's Experiment

This experiment was discussed at length in the previous chapter, and there the analysis of the data by the Unfolding Technique was presented. In summary, there were eight stimuli, as follows:

A — $ 800	E — $3300
B — 1300	F — 3900
C — 2000	G — 4400
D — 2600	H — 4800

which were administered by the Method of Paired Comparisons to 106 graduating seniors who judged each pair from the point of view of which member of the pair best represents what he thinks he will be worth to a prospective employer in his field in his first year after receiving his bachelor's degree. The results from unfolding revealed a common qualitative J scale for almost all the subjects with the stimuli in the alphabetical order given above. There was, on the other hand, no unique set of metric relations between these stimuli which would satisfy all the subjects. A solution for the metric relations which would satisfy a majority of the subjects was given, but there is not sufficient information in such data to yield a unique solution even if one existed.

The real purpose of this experiment was to obtain a Group scale by the Law of Comparative Judgment solution (Case V) to the paired comparisons and to compare this with the *theoretical* Group scale where the dollar values of the stimuli were assumed to correspond to their Q values. The C value of each individual was his answer to the question on page 30 of the questionnaire: what specific numerical value did you have in mind in making your judgments? With these numerical values taken as Q and C values respectively, by application of Statements 6, 8a, and 9a, the quantity P_{hij} could be computed for every triplet (h, i, j) and the quantity $P_{h \cdot j}$ calculated. The Law of Comparative Judgment solution, equivalent to Equation (79), should agree with these values within a linear transformation. The theoretical solution for the Group scale uses experimental data only from one question, indicated above, and is not based on any of the paired comparison data. The Law of Comparative Judgment solution is based exclusively on the paired comparison judgments of the individuals. The relation of these two analyses of the data is given in Figure 13.

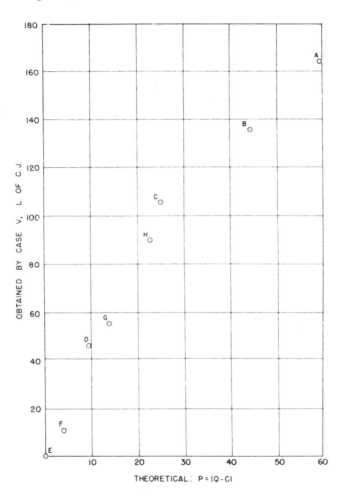

Figure 13.

It appears that a close relationship is indicated. Some error is to be anticipated from the assumptions involved in the Law of Comparative Judgment, Case V, and from the approximations involved in using dollar values as Q and C values. The Unfolding Technique revealed that arithmetic differences in dollars did not correspond to psychological magnitudes, nor for that matter did any other monotone function of the differences.

In passing, it may again be pointed out that the Law of Comparative Judgment solution for a Group scale in this case represents a Joint scale folded, as the Group scale has the stimuli in the order: EFGDHCBA, which is the J scale ABCDEFGH folded in the neighborhood of E.

The Lifted-Weight Experiment

It was the objective of this experiment to test quantitatively the relation between a Joint scale and a Group scale, i.e., Case II of the first Law of Comparative Judgment and the related postulates, and in addition Case II of the second Law of Comparative Judgment with its related postulates. In order to accomplish this second objective it was necessary that relatively indiscriminable stimuli be used in order that a solution by the Law of Comparative Judgment would be possible. For this reason lifted weights were used as stimuli with values as follows:

A	92 grams	F	102 grams
B	94	G	104
C	96	H	106
D	98	I	108
E	100	J	110

The design of this experiment is moderately complicated; there are three phases to this study based on two distinct experiments.

Phase 1 is an experiment on 50 subjects using the Method of Paired Comparisons, task A, and will be called experiment A. For this experiment there is both a theoretical solution and a Case V Law of Comparative Judgment solution which should be closely related.

Phase 2 is an experiment on a different set of 50 subjects, using the same stimuli, but the data were collected by the Method of Paired Comparisons, task B, and this experiment will be called experiment B. Here also there is both a theoretical and a Case V Law of Comparative Judgment solution which should be closely related.

Phase 3 involves a comparison of the two Case V Laws of Comparative Judgment solutions in phases 1 and 2.

86

Phase 1.

The first experiment, called experiment A, was a study of the first Law of Comparative Judgment, for data collected by the Method of Paired Comparisons, task A. This experiment corresponds identically to Cutler's except for the character of the stimuli. For experiment A there is both a theoretical solution based on the postulates using the logarithm of the gram weights to approximate Q and C values, and a Case V Law of Comparative Judgment solution based on the paired comparison judgments of the subjects. In such a domain as lifted weights individuals have no ideal of their own with respect to which a preference between two weights may be expressed. Consequently, in order to secure task A data, each individual in this experiment was given one of the weights to serve as his standard. The instructions to the examiner for the task A experiment are given below; they contain also the instructions to the subject:

Task A

To Examiner:

1) Conceal the weights not being used.

2) Conceal the record of choices. Make no comment about the judgments and do not tell or show the subject his results until the experiment is completed, and even then try to hold discussion to a minimum. In order to alleviate boredom, inform the subject two or three times as to how nearly done the experiment is.

3) Note the standard on the data sheet.

4) When the subject hands you the weight judged "nearer," record it by circling it on the data sheet and ret· n it to the rack. Then return the other weight to the rack. Always return both weights to the rack, even though one of them is to be used in the next judgment (to avoid giving any kind of clue to the subject).

5) Set the weights before the subject, one pair at a time in right and left position, *with respect to him,* as indicated on the data sheet.

6) Say to the subject: "This is a study of your perception of relative heaviness. I'll give you this weight to use as a standard. Keep it right side up, and lift it in this fashion (demonstrate) when making your comparisons. You will then be given weights in pairs, and your job is to determine which of the two in each pair is nearer the standard in weight. You will probably find it rather difficult to distinguish between the members of some pairs, and this has been arranged purposely, the judgment 'equal' is not allowed—you have to judge one to be nearer the standard. Take as much time as you wish and when you have made your decision, hand to me the weight you judge nearer. Any question about what you are to do? Here are the first two weights."

7) Record the time when the first pair of weights is presented.

8) Record the time when the subject makes his last judgment.

All stimuli were used as standard with equal frequency, there were five subjects for each. The Q values of the stimuli were assumed to be approximated by the logarithm of their weight in grams. The individuals' C values was the logarithm of the weight in grams of the stimulus assigned as a standard. The theoretical Group scale of "preferences" then, corresponding to Equation (79) was calculated without reference to the individuals' judgments. At the same time a Case V solution to the paired comparison judgments was computed, and these should be in reasonably close agreement. A plot of the two scales for the stimuli is given in Figure 14. The results indicate a fair relationship in view of the assump-

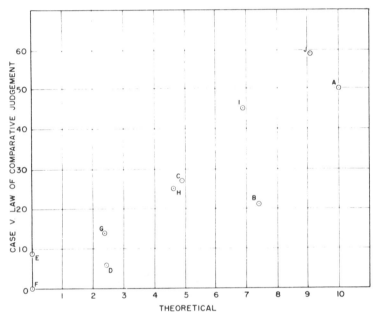

Figure 14.

tions and approximations that had to be introduced over and above the basic theory and in view of the fact that these data are based on 50 cases. The number of cases, of course, is irrelevant to the theoretical solution but important for the reliability of the Case V Law of Comparative Judgment solution. It would have been much better to have 200 cases, but this would have required 400 cases for the total experiment, and it took a full semester to collect the 50 cases for each of the two experiments described here.* The results on these cases are regarded as sufficiently indicative for the purpose of this study.

*The data for the lifted weight experiments were collected by three examiners, Mr. John Milholland, Mr. Richard Cutler, and Mrs. Joyce Newkirk.

Phase 2.

The second phase involved collecting paired comparison judgments task B from 50 subjects using the same 10 stimuli. The instructions to the examiner are given below:

Task B

To Examiner:

1) Conceal the weights not being used.

2) Conceal the record of choices. Make no comment about the judgments and do not tell or show the subject his results until the experiment is completed, and even then try to hold discussion to a minimum. In order to alleviate boredom, inform the subject two or three times as to how nearly done the experiment is.

3) When the subject hands you a weight judged heavier, record it by circling it on the data sheet and return it to the rack. Then return the other weight to the rack. Always return both weights to the rack, even though one of them is to be used in the next judgment (to avoid giving any kind of clue to the subject).

4) Set the weights before the subject, one pair at a time, in right and left position, *with respect to him*, as indicated on the data sheet.

5) Say to the subject: "This is a study of your perception of relative heaviness. You will be given weights in pairs such as these and you are asked to judge which one is heavier. Make your judgments by lifting the weights with your right hand if you are right handed, your left hand if you are left handed. Do not move your elbow up off the table and keep the weights right side up and vertical (demonstrate). Take as much time as you wish and when you have made your decision, hand the heavier one to me. You will probably find it rather difficult to distinguish between the members f some pairs, and this has been arranged purposely, but the judgment "equal" is not allowed—you have to judge one to be heavier. Do you have any question about what you are to do? Here are the first two weights."

6) Record the time when the first pair of weights is presented.

7) Record the time when the subject makes his last judgment.

A theoretical solution for the stimulus scale was obtained based on Statements 6, 8b, 9b, and 10c. The genotypic scale values (Q values) of the stimuli were assumed to be approximated by the logarithm of their weights in grams. On the basis of Statement 10c an individual was given a C value for the pair of weights that he was judging, equal to the mean of their Q values. This is equivalent to saying that for the Method of Paired Comparisons, task B, an individual takes a single C value for each pair of stimuli midway between their genotypic scale values. These genotypic values then permitted the computation of the phenotypic scale values P_{hij}, for each individual for every judgment. The final phenotypic scale of the stimuli of their "felt-heaviness" was then computed in accordance with equation 84, Case II of the second Law of Comparative

89

Judgment. This solution was obtained of course entirely from theory with no dependence on the data.

A Case V Law of Comparative Judgment solution was then obtained from the paired comparison judgments themselves. The agreement between these two solutions is illustrated in Figure 15. The relation is quite good.

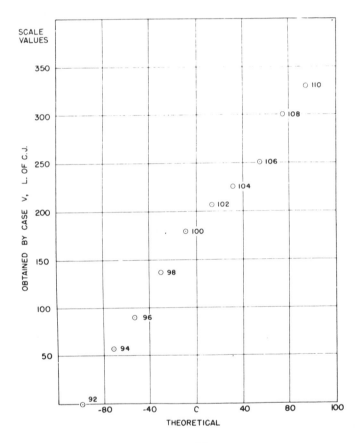

Figure 15.

Phase 3.

This phase consists of a comparison of the distances between stimuli on the empirical Stimulus scale (phase 2) with the distances obtained by unfolding the empirical Group scale (phase 1), the respective data having been obtained on different samples of subjects making judgments under different instructions. The scale values of the stimuli on the empirical Stimulus scale are the ordinates of the points in Figure 15. Distances between adjacent pairs of stimuli are readily computed from there. In a similar manner distances between corresponding pairs of stimuli on the Group scale may be obtained from Figure 14. Theoretically, one set of values should be a linear transformation of the other. The obtained relation is illustrated in Figure 16.

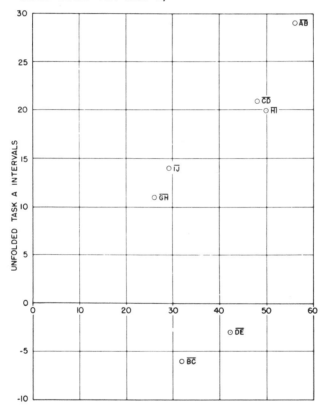

Figure 16.

It appears that five of the intervals satisfy a straight line but two are clearly off. It can be seen that this is the result of the fact that stimuli D and E on the empirical Group scale are in reverse order from theoretical expectations, and the same may be said for B and C. These two reversals may be a consequence of the fact that only 50 subjects were used in the experiment and the stimuli differ by only 2 grams.

It will be desirable to carry out more intensive experiments to study these relations more carefully.

BIBLIOGRAPHY

1. Anastasi, Anne, "The Nature of Psychological Traits," *Psychol. Rev.*, 1948, vol. 55, p. 127-138.
2. Anderson, J. E. "Freedom and Constraint or Potentiality and Environment," *Psychol. Bull.*, 1944, vol. 41, p. 1-29.
3. Arrow, Kenneth J. *Social Choice and Individual Values.* New York: John Wiley and Sons, 1951, 99 pp.
4. Bennett, J. F. *The Dimensionality of a Set of Rank Orders.* Ph. D. thesis. University of Michigan, 1951.
5. Bergmann, Gustav, and K. W. Spence. "The Logic of Psychological Measurement," *Psychol. Rev.*, 1944, vol. 51, p. 1-24.
6. Carnap, Rudolf. "Foundations of Logic and Mathematics," *Encyclopedia of Unified Science*, vol. 1, no. 3. Chicago: University of Chicago Press, 1939.
7. Coombs, C. H. "Some Hypotheses for the Analysis of Qualitative Variables," *Psychol. Rev.*, 1948, vol. 55, p. 167-174.
8. Coombs, C. H. "Psychological Scaling Without a Unit of Measurement," *Psychol. Rev.*, 1950, vol. 57, p. 145-158.
9. Coombs, C. H. "The Concepts of Reliability and Homogeneity," *J. Ed. Psychol. Meas.*, 1950, vol. 10, p. 43-56.
10. Coombs, C. H. "Mathematical Models in Psychological Scaling," *J. A. S. A.*, 1951, vol. 46, p. 480-489
11. Coombs, C. H. "The Theory and Methods of Social Measurement," in: *Research Methods in Social Psychology*, edited by L. Festinger and D. Katz. New York: Dryden Press, in press.
12. Guilford, J. P. *Psychometric Methods.* New York: McGraw-Hill, 1936.
13. Gulliksen, Harold. "Paired Comparisons and the Logic of Measurement," *Psychol. Rev.*, 1946, vol. 53, p. 199-213.
14. Guttman, Louis. Chapters 2, 3, 6, 8, 9 in: Samuel A. Stouffer, *et al. Measurement and Prediction.* Princeton: Princeton University Press, 1950.
15. Horst, A. P. "A Method for Determining the Absolute Affective Value of a Series of Stimulus Situations," *J. Ed. Psychol. Meas.*, 1932, vol. 23, p. 418-440.
16. Janis, Irving L. "Problems Related to the Control of Fear in Combat," Chapt. 4 in: S. A. Stouffer, *et al. The American Soldier. Vol. II. Combat and Its Aftermath.* Princeton: Princeton University Press, 1949.
17. Lazarsfeld, Paul F. Chapters 10, 11 in: Samuel A. Stouffer, *et al. Measurement and Prediction.* Princeton: Princeton University Press, 1950.
18. Marschak, Jacob. "Rational Behavior, Uncertain Prospects, and Measurable Utility," *Econometrica*, 1950, vol. 18, p. 111-141.
19. Mosteller, Frederick. "Remarks on the Method of Paired Comparisons: I. The Least Squares Solution Assuming Equal Standard Deviations and Equal Correlations," *Psychometrika*, 1951, vol. 16, p. 3-9.

20. Nagel, Ernest. *On the Logic of Measurement*. Ph. D. thesis. Columbia University, 1930.

21. Stevens, S. S. "On the Theory of Scales of Measurement," *Science*, 1946, vol. 103, p. 677-680.

22. Thurstone, L. L. "A Law of Comparative Judgment," *Psychol. Rev.*, 1927, vol. 34, p. 273-286.

23. Thurstone, L. L. "An Experimental Study of Nationality Preferences," *J. Gen. Psychol.*, 1928, vol. 1, p. 405-424.

24. von Neumann, J., and O. Morgenstern. *Theory of Games and Economic Behavior*. 2nd ed., Princeton: Princeton University Press, 1947. 641 pp.

25. Woodger, J. H. "The Technique of Theory Construction," *International Encyclopedia of Unified Science*, vol. 2, no. 5, p. 6 ff. Chicago: University of Chicago Press, 1939.